# The Architecture of India
Buddhist and Hindu

# The Architecture of India
## Buddhist and Hindu

## Satish Grover

Exclusive Distributor
for USA and CANADA
**Advent Books, Inc.**
141 East 44th Street
New York, NY 10017

**VIKAS PUBLISHING HOUSE PVT LTD**
VIKAS HOUSE, 20/4 Industrial Area, Sahibabad
Distt. Ghaziabad, U.P. (India)

VIKAS PUBLISHING HOUSE PVT LTD
*Regd. Office* : 5 Ansari Road, New Delhi 110002
*Head Office* : VIKAS HOUSE, 20/4 Industrial Area, Sahibabad, Distt. Ghaziabad, U.P. (India)
*Branches* : Savoy Chambers 5 Wallace Street, Bombay/10 First Main Road, Gandhi Nagar, Bangalore/8/1-B Chowringhee Lane, Calcutta/80 Canning Road, Kanpur

COPYRIGHT © SATISH GROVER, 1980

1V2G5102
ISBN 0-7069-0685-3

Printed at Delhi Press, New Delhi.

*For Razia whose silent but persistent
support made this book possible*

# Acknowledgements

During the years that this book has been in the thinking, writing and making, I have received help, inspiration and criticism from many. Let me express my gratitude, in chronological order, in which much of this book has been written. To Ranjit Sabikhi who as guru during my student days opened our eyes to the architectural wealth of India; friend Ratna Sahai who spent hours turning the first draft of the manuscript inside out to make literary sense out of architectural notes; the ageless B.L. Mehta who so ungrudgingly typed and retyped the script but has not lived to see it in print; S.K. Singh, Salman Haider and Prof Jhabwala for professional suggestions; Krishna Sikund who added a touch of dash to the prose; the staff of the Photo Section of the Archaelogical Survey of India, New Delhi, for providing most of the photographs; Mr S. L. Sharma of the School of Planning and Architecture, New Delhi, for photographic assistance; to Poonam Grover for so patiently drawing most of the sketches that illustrate the text; N.C. Menon for retyping the final manuscript; and Neelam Mehta for correcting the proofs.

## ACKNOWLEDGEMENTS OF ILLUSTRATIONS

Archaeological Survey of India: Figs—2, 3, 5, 6, 8, 9, 17, 31, 68, 85, 89, 105, 124, 126, 127, 138, 139, 144, 180.

Brown, Percy: Figs—12, 13, 13a, 41, 43, 48, 60, 70, 78, 86, 96, 110, 171, 211, 213

Volwhasen, A.: Figs—15, 116, 189, 203

# Preface

It took the reading of many prefaces to understand the meaning and intention of one. Having understood a preface to be a *raison d'être* for writing a book, it does not seem like such an onerous task. To begin chronologically, I must go back a few years to my days as a student of architecture in the Delhi School.

Though I have never been averse to travel I really caught the bug of professional travel during a college-sponsored tour of Rajasthan, Gujarat and Saurashtra. The historic architecture of the many regions of India has since remained a constant source of nourishment for me and the fascination with India and its people an undying one. A book, then, on the History of Indian Architecture seemed an ideal project for giving concrete expression to both emotions. And, finally, I hope I have managed to capture in words the first half of the subcontinent's history in the craft of building.

The format of the book is once again based on three immediate aspects of my own life—as a professional architect, as a lecturer in the History of Indian Architecture, and as an urbanite with an urbanite's usual quota of social interaction. The book is aimed at being interesting reading for all the three sections of people. Courses in history of architecture in professional schools have, for better or worse, moved completely away from a detailed study of individual buildings or merely of "classified" styles to a broader understanding of architectural phenomena in their social context. The professional modern architect is also more interested in understanding the mind of the "guru-architect," the techniques of the craftsmen and the development of design ideas that resulted in the masterpieces of the past rather than in mere elaborate descriptions of individual monuments. The inquisitive urbanite too would like his monuments placed in historical perspective and need, maybe, some guidance in appreciating the aesthetic achievements of the builders, rather than be overburdened with technical jargon and voluminous tomes classifying each of the millions of structures into varying styles.

The book is intended to provide sufficient reading for the student of architecture to be able to probe more detailed writings on the subject with sufficient confidence; to break down the cynicism of the practising modern Indian architect to the country's architectural heritage and to arm the more inquisitively inclined tourist of India with sufficient background material to appreciate the essence of Indian architecture. To achieve the above, it has been necessary to take some liberties from the "classic" way of writing a book on historical architecture. In this, as far as possible, I have followed chronology, for I believe that few incidents of history can be treated as isolated phenomena. In spite of the poor communication systems of the past, every human act in one part of the world is somehow derived from another, and interconnected with yet another. A study of history is meaningful only because it is so. The same principle is applicable to the history of architecture.

In the Indian context, I have emphasised this by relating the development of architectural ideas to the passage of time rather than to mere geographical locations. At the same time, one cannot gainsay the fact that due to historical circumstances there have been occasions when blossoming of a "style" has depended for its nourishment on narcistic rather than universal knowledge. The chronological chase then has had to be momentarily given up in favour of the geographical and dynastic one. A need though to explain either phenomena against a socio-historical backdrop is common to both, for which the reader has been provided with sufficient material.

Another fact that has been emphasised and should be of interest to the reader—particularly the contemporary architect—is that the builders of the past were grappling with problems in much the same way as we architects today. They had their own brand of professional pride, their own set of "clients" to satisfy their own problems of meeting their economic needs and at the same time rationally structuring edifices to meet the "gothic" or "baroque" needs of the clients and the social times. The parallel situation I hope will be made transparent in a chapter exclusively devoted to describing the virtual "trade unions" of historical India, and the Vastupurushamandala, that forms the geomantic, theological and academic backbone of ancient Hindu architecture.

SATISH GROVER

## Contents

INTRODUCTION ... xi

1. INDUS VALLEY CIVILIZATION ... 1
   Urbanity in Mohenjodaro

2. ARYAN IMMIGRATION AND THE VEDIC PERIOD ... 13
   Magic chants in bamboo villages

3. BUDDHA, MAHAVIRA AND THE MAURYAS ... 21
   The "Garden City" of Pataliputra

4. THE AHIMSA OF ASOKA THE GREAT ... 27
   The Stupa, the Stambha and the Vedika

5. THE SHUNGAS, THE MERCHANTS AND THE BUDDHISTS ... 37
   "Heavenly domes" of Sanchi

6. THE ANDHRAS OF THE SOUTH ... 47
   Stupa of Amravati and caves of Karli

7. THE GREEKS, KUSHANS AND THE "LARGER VEHICLE" ... 59
   The guilded shrines of Gandhara

8. THE "SANSKRIT" BRAHMINISM OF THE GUPTAS ... 69
   Sombre "Garbha-Grihas" and joyous Ajanta

9. THE CHALUKYAS AND THE GUPTAS ... 81
   Brahmin shrines—North and South

10. HARSHA—THE LAST GREAT BUDDHIST ... 93
    Sarnath, Gaya and Nalanda

11. THE CHALUKYA PALLAVA POWER BALANCE ... 101
    Shrines of Aihole, Badami and Mahabalipuram

12. THE TRIUMPHANT PALLAVAS AND RASHTRAKUTAS ... 111
    Building at Kanchipuram and carving at Ellora

13. THE FEUDAL NORTH ... 125
    Temples in Rajasthan and Kashmir

14. Rajput "Vanshas" and the Kalinga Kings    139
    Classicism at Gwalior and Bhubaneswar

15. The Chandelas of Bundelkhand    149
    Khajuraho's Jagadambi and Puri's Jagannath

16. The Hindu Jaina Axis of Gujarat    159
    "Mandapa" temples in the West

17. The Mystique of the "Vastupurushamandala"    171
    The Theories of Hindu Architecture

18. The Splendours of Medieval India    181
    The "cathedrals" of Modhera, Konarak and Khajuraho

19. Cholas and Pandyas, The Magnificent Tamils    193
    Tanjore and soaring Gopurams

20. The Hoysalas of the Karnataka    203
    "Star" Temples in Halebid and Belur

21. Vijayanagar—The last great glory    215
    Architecture of Hampi

22. Nayaks of the Deep South    223
    Temple cities of Madurai and Rameswaram

Bibliography    233
Glossary    235
Index    237

# Introduction

Until history repeats itself and another discovery as significant and startling as that of the existence of the Indus Valley Civilization is made, any history of Indian architecture must inevitably begin from the time when the earliest known wave of immigrants settled in modern Sind and Punjab. They planned and built the now famous cities of Mohenjodaro and Harappa between 3000 and 2000 B.C. Not only are these the earliest extant remains of recognizable building activity in India, there is a discernible link in the traditions of the Indus Valley and that of the latter-day Hindus—this in spite of the best and most deliberate efforts of the later Aryans to decimate the urban centres of the civilization. The Brahmins of medieval India, for example, were different from the Harappan "priest-kings" in so far that the temporal powers of the time had been usurped by the militant Kshatriya caste, leaving the Brahmin a mere "priest" and not king too; the bathing tank of Mohenjodaro is surely the earliest prototype of the inevitable sacred pool of any temple city of 15th century Dravida; and there is, of course, the mother Goddess cult-worship that certainly carried over as Durga into the "classified list" of the pantheon of Hindu gods.

Architecturally speaking, the link is more tenous and staccato. From the brick architecture of the Indus Valley, we are plunged into the Vedic period of bamboo and timber hamlets and only a bit more gradually into the enduring cave and stone architecture of the Buddhist and medieval Hindus. The continuity prevails, however, in the all-pervading standardisation in the techniques of building and town planning of the Harappans' and the equally inviolate Brahmin laws of theology and geometry that permeate the sculptured architectural surfaces of Hindu temples all over India. The link-up, then, with the Harappan civilization is more of the "mind" than of actual expression. The "physical connection" though is apparent from the Vedic period of about 500 B.C. right up to 16th century Hindu India.

Thus, though the forms of the thatch and bamboo huts of the Vedic village are strikingly fragile compared to the brick houses of the urban Harappan, these fragile rural forms of Aryan India were immortalised by being hewn out of enduring stone in the later periods. It is this transmutation of architectural ideas from one material to another, from one religion to another, from one people to another and from one region to another, that forms the core of this history.

No actual example of timber architecture of the Vedic period of over 3000 years ago has, of course, survived the ravages of time. Our information, though, of this period is based on the "concrete" evidence left behind by the latter-day Buddhist sculptor who adorned his stone monuments with a visual relief of the legendary tales of its founder, set against the background of the Indian countryside of the Vedic period. In the renowned bas reliefs of Sanchi, for example, we see clusters of circular huts with domical thatch roofs, gable, arched timber palaces and loggias, the ornate projecting timber balconies and arcuated openings that permeated the streets of Aryan villages and trading towns with a *joie de vivre* lacking in the workmanlike and windowless streets of Mohenjodaro and Harappa.

We turn, thereafter, to the influence of the great teachers —Buddha and Mahavira—who obviously did not share in the great "joy" of the Aryan. In fact, they riddled holes into the fabric of his society by pointing out the social evils inherent in his degrading "caste system", in his tolerance of primitive Tantric rights as a means of salvation; in the glorifying of the violence of tribal Aryan wars; in its surrounding religion in an aura of Sanskrit mumbo-jumbo and elaborate ritual incomprehensible to the rural Aryan. The common Indian, then, flocked with relief to listen to the simple and straightforward sermons of these two apostles of peace, instead of being mute witnesses to the great sacrificial *yagnas* of the Brahmins.

One of the apostles, Buddha, was fortunate in finding a great patron in none other than Emperor Ashoka. This fortuitous event in 326 B. C. marks the beginning of the longest and most enduring part of the history of Indian architecture— that of the use of stone as a building material. Ashoka took his cue from the contemporary Persian stone masons who had already built the marvellous stone palaces of Darius and Xerxes, and set up schools of stone craftsmanship, most likely supervised by Persian gurus. The graduates from these colleges ultimately built monuments of stone to the enduring glory of Ashoka's state-patronised religion of Buddhism. Toranas, chaityas, stupas, stambhas, and vedikas dotted the countryside of Buddhist India of the Ashokan period. Crafted in stone as they were, these monuments are witness to the Buddhist masons' skills in the "carpentry of stone."

The Buddhist monks, however, seem to have had little confidence in the endless survival even of these stone monuments. As they retired to isolated plateaus and mountains to meditate in peace, they decided to enlarge and transform the natural grottos and caves of the hillsides into great and glorious prayer halls and monasteries for their clergy. They were now certain that as long as the gorges and cliffs of Ajanta, Ellora, and Karle survived the monuments of Buddhism too would not vanish. In carving out these "wonderous caverns of light" out of the granite hillsides, they added a new and unique dimension to the Indian architectural tradition that, for lack of more appropriate nomenclature, has been termed "cave architecture." There is no parallel to the aesthetic achievements of the Buddhist "rock architects" in any other order of architecture anywhere in the world.

India's freedom from the tentacles of Brahminism, though glorious, was shortlived. Ironically, the first victim of the Brahmins subtle machinations were the Buddhist clergy. In deifying the "Buddha" as "saviour," whose image could be worshipped like that of Hindu gods, the protagonists of Mahayana Buddhism played themselves into the all-absorbing pantheon of Hindu gods. The Brahmin was only too keen to accept Gautama the Buddha as an avtar of Brahma, as long as Brahma alone was recognised as the Supreme One. The lesson of the priest kings of the Indus Valley too was not forgotten by the Brahmin. He realised the necessity of setting up an alliance with the Kshatriya's—the Aryan purveyors of temporal power—who were "raring" to go to bloody war and re-live the glorious days of the Mahabharata, the messages of Buddha and Mahavira notwithstanding. The rather pessimistic tone of Buddhism and the great material prosperity of 5th century India paved the path for the resurgence of Brahminism under the great dynasty of the Guptas. Once re-established, Hindu hegemony has not relented its hold over the majority of the Indian people for well over a millenium.

It is of course the architectural output of this great resurgence that we are concerned with; an architectural tradition that, after fumbling through an early period of uncertain experimentation with the forms of a Hindu "place of worship," in towns like Aihole and Badami (in modern Karnataka), emerged confident and triumphant to build the great temple-cathedrals of Konarak, Gujarat, Khajuraho and Tanjore.

In arriving at this stage of confidence, the Hindu designer took a long and tortuous journey, the rewards of which, though, seem to justify the effort. Just like Ashokan craftsmen had fashioned the Vedic timber forms into *toranas* and *stambhas*, the builder of the Hindu temple took his cue from rural folk forms as well as extant Buddhist structures. The result of the former was the Shikhara and of the latter the Vimana. Ultimately these two towering forms became the distinguishing features of the north and south Indian style of temple architecture. The raw masonry forms of the Shikhara and Vimana that thus emerged at Aihole, Badami and Pattadakal were ultimately refined by the skill of the sculptors of Mahabalipuram who fashioned a series of experimental dummy sancturies out of an outcrop of living rock. Ultimately, through interaction between the cave carvers of Ajanta and Elephanta, the Rashtrakuta and Pallava rock cutters of Ellora and Mahabalipuram, the Chalukyan stone masons of Badami and the Gupta bricklayers of Bhitargaon, emerged the crystallisation of the two mother-styles—the northern and the southern.

Though identifiable schools of art—the north Indian or Indo-Aryan and the South Indian or Dravidian (as classified by traditional writers),—and the rather hybrid form of Jaina architecture emerged, the "priest architect" retained enough academic control over his Hindu craftsmen to ensure the essential design unity of the architecture of India—North, South, East or West. In order to trace and illustrate this unity, one has to bridge from one centre of architectural activity in one corner of India to another. From the Shikharas, Vimanas and Samosans of Osian, Tanjore and Dilwara to the Gudha *mandapa*, Nat Mandir and Pradakshina Paths of Modhera, Orissa and Khajuraho, to the Prakrams, trefoil arches and *rathas* of Rameswaram, Kashmir and Konarak; all built by the burgeoning feudal lords to the great glory of Shiv, Brahma and Vishnu in the plains, plateaus, mountains and hillsides of India. Until the wheel, so to say, comes full circle, once again in the region of modern Karnataka, not far from Badami, the original birthplace of the Hindu temple.

Here in the cities of Halebid and Belur, the so-called northern and southern style are submerged once again into a single entity in the great creations of the Hoysaleswara's. The rectangular offsets of the pyramidical form of the Vimana and the curvilinear profile of the Shikhara are transmuted into a bell shaped tower planted over a star shaped *garbhagriha*. The surfaces of the productions of the master architect, Acharya Janaka, are adorned with the most profusely decorated sculptures of Devas and Apsaras overshadowing even the sensuous forms of the famous erotica of Khajuraho in its flourishes and ornamentation.

Hereinafter, leaving the north, which earlier in 12th century had already succumbed to Islam, we witness spasmodic artistic outbursts of the genius of the southern people, who were virtually on the run from the inexorable march of Islam. The last monumental if not innovative outcome of their talents was the legendary city of Vijayanagar or Hampi, the ruins of which confirm the glorious descriptions of it recorded by the many visitors to the city in its heyday. Thereafter, we are left only with the fortress-like temple cities of the deep south. The cities of Madurai, Srirangam, and Rameswaram do greater justice to the perseverance and indefatigability of the Hindu builder, than to his architectural genius. Miles upon miles of corridors, halls upon halls of millions of columns, rings around rings of battlemented walls, towering *gopurams* after *gopurams* are the essentials of this "style"–if it may be called one. The progressive and assimilative genius of the Indian builder seems to have dried up under the orthodox and plebian demands of his chief client—the Hindu priest—who seems to have been preoccupied with protecting his religion and archaic social systems from the invigiorating influences of Islam.

History had finally caught up with India again. Another of the seemingly endless and periodic invasions of India—this time that of the Muslims—finally and mercifully called a halt to the humdrum activity of throwing concentric walls and *mandapas* of florid columns around the ancient temples of southern India.

How the invaders tapped the Indian builders' resources in giving a new lease of life to architecture in India, by building great and glorious mosques, palaces and tombs is another story.

# 1

## Indus Valley Civilization

### Urbanity in Mohenjodaro

MORE than 5000 years ago, an itinerant group of people probably of Sumerian origin, wandered into the northwest of India by way of the Mula Pass and the coastal road which runs through Las Bela and Makran and crosses the Hab near modern Karachi (Fig. 1). Fortuitously, may be they had found their way into a breath-taking green valley, richly forested, and abundantly watered by the now legendary river Sindhu. Travelling further up the river, they discovered the alluvial plains of the fabled "land of the five rivers"; Sindh, Jhelum, Chenab, Ravi and Sutlej (later day Punjab). To these wayfarers across the deserts of Iran, this land was God's own gift. There was no reason to wander further; the rivers assured them a dependable supply of water and the banks were ideal for cultivation. The forests around were not only an abundant source of game but timber as well; timber that could be used as building material, as fuel for cooking and even, as they were to soon learn, for baking bricks to build permanent structures.

Over a period of almost a thousand years the proliferating clans of these immigrants had spread themselves over an area of about half a million square miles along and around the river valley. The paraphernalia of urban life generated during this period is the substance of the earliest known civilization of India—that of the Indus Valley. Founded more

1. Routes of entry of immigrants into India from the Iranian plateau, Afghanistan, and China. Left, a conjectural restoration of the city of Mohenjodaro.

than two and half milleniums before the birth of Christ, the civilization marks not only the beginning of the art of building in India, but was destined to be the crucible of Indian culture, as we know it today.

During the first millenium of their settlement in the valley, the people most likely lived in clearings reclaimed from the forests on the banks of the river. Nature was bountiful to them and resources of the environment seemed inexhaustible and abundant. With their knowledge of cultivation not only of rice and wheat but also cotton as well, probably by a system of irrigation, the community was able to produce sufficient agricultural surplus without undue strain. Such self-sufficiency in basic necessities encouraged the growth of industries like pottery, brick-making, carpentry and weavings of cotton textiles. Consequently, a prosperous mercantile class, also engaged in overseas trade, emerged. It was only natural for such a peaceable and rich community involved in multifarious activities to congregate in settlements of an urban nature.

## PRIEST KINGS AND CITY STATES

Inhabitants of the Indus Valley soon discovered, however, that the very elements which sustained their lives, could also become great forces of destruction. The forest, an abundant source of timber for building and fuel, abounded too with wild life; crocodiles, tigers, elephants and rhinoceroses. It was an unknown and untamed source of threat to human life. Otherwise life giving rivers were also liable to devastatingly damaging floods. The common folks meagre knowledge of these phenomena, and an equally meagre technology to combat these forces, encouraged a section of the people to set themselves up as a semi-divine priestly class. This group were the "magic men" who claimed that they could contain the vast forces of nature, and control the environment that appeared hostile, by elaborate rituals of appeasement of the gods above. Gradually, but surely, the self-styled priest like the latter day Hindu Brahmins gained control over the various aspects of the life of these people. They became, in fact, virtual priest kings, exercising both spiritual and temporal authority. The organisation, through which this authority was exercised, may have been a group of peacefully coexisting city states or even a single large empire.

**2.** A small residential block in Mohenjodaro within the grid of main and subsidiary streets.

**2a.** Shaded area showing excavated area within the mile square layout of Mohenjodaro.

## ARCHAEOLOGICAL EXCAVATIONS

The script used by the people of the Indus Valley, consisting of some 270 symbols, remains undeciphered. Historical processes in the Indus Valley have left us with neither a "Papyrus scrolls" nor a "Rosetta Stone" as a clue. Conclusive evidence is available only to the fact that they wrote from the left to the right. Our knowledge of their culture is, therefore, based entirely on archaeological excavations carried out as late as the 19th century, which brought to light the various settlements and cities of the civilization. These and subsequent excavations have revealed that the community had spread over a vast area. Colonies were located even as far down as Lothal in Gujarat state of present day India. Nevertheless, the 1000 miles (1600 km) long valley of the Indus and its tributaries, was the spine of the civilization. At the northern and southern ends of it, stood two major seats of government. These were the similarly laid out, now famous, cities of Harappa and Mohenjodaro. The two cities were located at the focii of an ellipse; the geographic ellipse apparently produced the agricultural surplus that sustained the dwellers of the cities. The urbanites in turn, produced and controlled the distribution of industrial goods and even carried on an overseas trade with the contemporary civilizations of modern Afganistan, Iran and Mesopotamia.

## THE CITIES OF HARAPPA AND MOHENJODARO

The planning, building and civic administration of their principal cities constitute the greatest achievement of the people of the Indus Valley. Unlike other ancient cities such as Sargom of Akkad, the towns of Harappa and Mohenjodaro were not the result of haphazard expansion of unplanned settlements. Rather these were built as carefully planned integral units (Fig. 2). Considering that this was one of man's earliest attempts at organizing his urban environment, the Indus Valley cities are outstanding examples of extremely effective town planning. For any comparable achievements in history, one would have to look almost 2500 years later, to the cantonment towns of the Roman empire.

Both, Mohenjodaro and Harappa were nearly a square-mile in plan (Fig. 2a) set within cranellated defensive walls. The layout of either town was a grid-iron pattern of streets about 30 feet (9 metres) wide, running in the north-south and east-west directions. The streets divided the city into 12 blocks, each measuring approximately $1200' \times 800'$ (365 m $\times$ 244 m). Apart from the central western blocks, the remaining were largely residential. The basic unit of the latter was a house of varying size and storeys, constructed with brick walls, roofed by brick tiles laid over timber rafters. It was planned as a series of rooms around an open-to-sky central court (Fig. 3). From the main streets the residents approached the individual houses through irregular, narrow and shaded walkways. The residential unit invariably had no entrances opening directly to the main streets (Fig. 5) and even no windows towards the subsidiary walkways. It depended for its light and ventilation entirely on the open central court, very much like most traditional housing in India even today.

3. Isometric projections of a typical conjecturally restored brick house of Mohenjodaro.

**4.** A typical community well in the residential area of the city of Mohenjodaro.

Groups of these units (Fig. 4) shared a common well for their water supply, though each house had its own separate bathing area. The entire city was served by an extensive system of drainage, the bathrooms being connected to drains running under the walkways which in turn were connected to large sewers laid out under the main street. While the smaller drains were covered with brick slabs, the larger main sewers were spanned over by corbelled brick arches. Manholes were located at regular intervals along the main sewer for inspection and cleaning of the drains. Such an elaborate drainage system, took care also of the abundant rainfall in the region, which at that time was not the virtual desert that it is today.

**5.** The typical residential unit at Mohenjodaro was built around an open-to-sky court without any windows opening on to streets.

# THE CITY CITADEL

For religious or other reasons, it was always the central blocks located on the western side that comprised the priestly citadel. At Mohenjodaro, it was built over a platform of baked bricks over 50 feet (15 metres) higher than the general level of the city. Within it were located a palace, a bathing tank and a massive granary. Since safe storage of grain was of the utmost importance to the economy of Mohenjodaro, the granary stood on the steep verge of the citadel. Half way up the northern end of it, a huge unloading platform was erected. Sheaves of grain were hoisted up from here to a timber shed which was built over twenty seven separate massive blocks of masonry. This left sufficiently large criss crossed ventilating ducts, running at the base of the shed (Fig. 8).

The citadel also had terraces at various levels approached by ramps or staircases, which were probably designed as processional paths for the rituals conducted by the priests. Within the citadel are also the ruins of a vast hall measuring

6. Isometric projections showing the great tank as it may have existed 5000 years ago.

7. Ruins of the great bathing tank as excavated at the site of Mohenjodaro.

8. Conjectural restoration of the granary at Mohenjodaro showing timber superstructure built over ventilating ducts and a brick masonry substructure.

230′ × 78′ (70 × 24 metres) which could have been either a palace or place of worship. A tank, meant obviously for ceremonial bathing, measuring 23′ × 39′ × 8′ (7 × 12.1 × 2.4 metres) deep, was meticulously waterproofed with asphalt and provided with an adequate system for filling and draining. Surrounding it was a series of cells which may have been living apartments for the priests (Fig. 6). The tank itself is obviously the prototype of the ritualistic bathing tanks, which are an inevitable part of the later Hindu temples (Fig. 7) of medieval times. Close to the citadel and the granaries were located circular brick paved flourmaking platforms, and a row of two-room barracks, apparently to house the labourers.

The timber superstructure of the granaries and the monumental architecture of the citadel has virtually vanished. The houses of Harappa and Mohenjodaro have been frequently described as "starkly utilitarian"; a judgement based on the assumption that the Indus Valley people did not decorate the excavated brick shells of their houses with ornamental timber work and painting. Judging from the artistic quality of their statuettes, toys, seals and jewellery, this is highly improbable. Even the empty shells of these houses indicate that the builders of the Indus Valley had intuitively evolved a system of planning for their houses, the essentials of which are eminently applicable even today to the life style that is Indian.

The open-to-sky courtyard around which the house was built, solved very effectively the problems of urban housing in a hot and dry climate. The central court could ventilate and light all rooms surrounding it, making openings into the street unnecessary and thereby affording the requisite privacy. It also provided a space for open air living within the house in which the harshness of the tropical sun was duly controlled (Fig. 9). The efficacy of this planning system is proved by the fact that right up to the 19th century, before the advent of British rule in India, this was the accepted system of house-building in Indian cities.

9. Right, the isometric projections of a restored house and left, the unearthed ruins of a typical Indus Valley street with blank windowless walls of houses on either side

## SECULAR AND RELIGIOUS ART

The urbane Indus valley people were also an artistically inclined people. Though the larger part of their art as discovered is of a secular nature, it is most probable that some sort of religious objects such as statues and magic symbols were made for rituals conducted by the priests. These were probably made of perishable material, and may even have been purposely destroyed to prevent these sacred objects from falling into the hands of invaders.

The remains of the secular art consist of jewellery such as ear-rings, pendants, belts, bangles, made in gold, silver and jade. The most interesting and also informative works of what may be called commercial art, are the numerous steatite seals. Square, rectangular and sometimes even circular (Fig. 10) measuring 2 or 3 cms, these were sawn out of steatite and exquisitely drawn figures of animals were then sunk in with small chisels. The seals were used for security and for identification of the ownership of property. The people were also familiar with the art of sculpture. Apart from statues made of steatite (Fig. 11) alabaster and limestone, images in copper and bronze were also moulded.

10. One of the steatite seals used for security and identification of ownership of property.

## STRATIFICATION AND DECAY

Having developed a surprisingly high standard of building, town planning and urban living, the Indus Valley people gradually got stratified into an intensely conservative and non-progressive group. It was as though once the mould of the city had jelled, the physical fact led to stasis. Although the cities of Mohenjodaro and Harappa were destroyed several times over, they were rebuilt on the foundations of the earlier cities with little variation in the overall plan. All techniques and activities were governed by severe standards The plans of cities like Mohenjodaro, Harappa, Kalibangan, Lothal and Rupar, though thousands of miles away from each other and set in different environments are almost identical varying only in size and detail. All the buildings of the cities were built with bricks of standard pattern and size of $5\frac{1}{2}'' \times 5\frac{1}{2}'' \times 11''$ ($12 \times 12 \times 27$ cms).

Over a period of 1000 years, there seems to have been little technological progress. Though the merchants traded with the contemporary overseas civilization, they seem to have been reluctant to borrow any new ideas from them. In terms of personal progress they seem to have isolated themselves completely. For a long period of time they lived without experiencing any wars. So peaceful was their existence that they never felt the need for developing any kind of armaments to defend themselves against human invasions. Only the forces of nature were to be confronted and the onus for this had been taken over by the priests. The most powerful of the natural forces were the recurring floods of the Indus. These they tried to overcome partly by acts of rebuilding, and partly by erecting dams on the rivers. But largely, it would seem, by their faith in the ritualistic mumbo-jumbo of the priest-kings. Gradually, their rapacious exploitation of nature and the wearisome task of repeatedly building their flood devastated cities year after year, began to sap the vigour of the civilization.

Ultimately around 1600 B.C. the cities were threatened from the West. A nomadic group of people riding horse and chariots poured down into the valley and found it as attractive as it had been to the original settlers, a millenium earlier. To these warlike invaders, the virtually unarmed people of the Indus Valley were easy prey. In the face of the invasion, rituals of the priests proved ineffective and their technological isolation made meaningful military retaliation impossible. After thriving for over a millenia, Mohenjodaro and Harappa were on the defensive. During the last years of their existence, they became virtually besieged cities, under constant threat from marauding tribal raids. New building activity naturally came to a stand-still. Additional living space was contrived by roofing over the central open courts of the houses. The stately wide avenues were encroached upon not only by the extensions of houses, but even brick kilns, which were now unsafe to site outside the city limits. The priest-kings were obviously finding it difficult to enforce the laws of the civilization any longer. Fully aware of the threat to their city, the rulers of Mohenjodaro, it would seem, were able to do little more than wall up the western gates of their city and in the ultimate reckoning flee for their lives from the invading hordes. The fall of Mohenjodaro, almost 3,500 years ago, signalled the decay of the entire civilization and its rapid subjugation by the invaders.

In terms of the development of building crafts in India this was indeed a great setback. As we shall see, another thousand years were to pass before the planners and builders of the invading group were able to achieve anything approaching the civil administration and town planning of the Indus Valley civilization.

11. A statue in steatite probably potraying one of the priest-kings.

# 2

# Aryan Immigration and the Vedic Period

## Magic chants in bamboo villages

IT is fairly certain now, that the hordes who subjugated the civilization of the Indus Valley were a people calling themselves Aryas, whose original home was somewhere in the legendary steppes of central Europe. Waves upon waves of Aryans in search of more favourable climes had been descending to the plains of Mesopotamia and the plateau of Iran. A group of these had for some time settled in the Iranian plateau. They were eventually driven further eastward by the pressure of subsequent immigration, and settled temporarily in Bactria, north-west of the Hindukush. Being nomadic warriors in search of green pastures, the country of Bactria did not hold them for long; soon they descended upon the primitive village settlements of Baluchistan. Hereafter, the conquest of the city states of an exhausted Indus Valley civilization was only a natural step in their march eastward.

The decimated urban settlements of the Indus Valley offered no attractions to the Aryan nomads. On the contrary, the cities seem to have aroused their contempt and wrath. Their later mythology alludes to the supreme warrior god Indra, breaking the brick and earthen protective dams, to destroy the cities by flooding them. The survivors of Aryan wrath on the Indus Valley inhabitants were reduced to impoverishment.

Some of them lingered on, as the Jhaluka and Jhukar squatters, on the remains of cities like Chanhudaro. Many seem to have migrated south to inhabit peninsular India, while a countless number may have been absorbed into the lowest social rung of the conquering Aryans. Abandoning the urban settlements of the Indus Valley to the ravages of nature, a large number of the invaders advanced further in search of richer, more virgin territories. They pushed eastward, through the natural corridor between the Thar Desert and the Himalayan foothills, and finally descended into the Gangetic plains in about 1500 B.C. The richly forested plain, with its rivers and vast banks of alluvial land unencumbered by permanent urban settlements. was just what the Aryans were looking for. The natural wealth of the area had hardly been touched upon by its original inhabitants; a scattering of non-agriculturist itenerant tribes. Word of the miracles engrained in the soil of the Gangetic plain spread fast and Aryan immigration into this area began at a furious pace.

12. A conjectural restoration of the 500 BC gate and city of Kusingara near Magadha in Bihar.

# WAR WITH THE ABORIGINALS

The Aryans attacked the "noseless and dark" aboriginals of the Gangetic plain with a ferocity no less than that of the later American white in conquering the Red Indians. With their military superiority, emphasised by horses and chariots, Aryan success was inevitable. Within a short period of time the invaders had spread themselves out in the Doab, the land between the two rivers of the Ganga and Jamuna, and foothills of the Himalaya and Vindhya mountains. The common foe, the so called *Dasyus* (literally "slave") having either been vanquished or enslaved, the Aryan, like the earlier Indus Valley settler, began living in small villages, on land reclaimed from the forests on the banks of rivers. The fertility of the land of the valley of the Ganga catalysed the transformation of the pastoral habits and the economic and social organization of the Aryans; the restless nomad was gradually weaned away from his wanderings and lured into the stable and established life of an agriculturist.

# THE ARYAN VILLAGE

Though the early Aryans had seen the use of brick in the cities of the Harappans, their descendants chose to build their village settlements in timber, bamboo and thatch, which were readily and abundantly available from the forests. The chariot builder of the fighting Aryan tribes was familiar with their use and was able to adapt his skills of carpentry easily to the building of wooden structures. Timber and bamboo dwellings were also simpler and easier to maintain or rebuild in case of damage by rains and floods. The new settler was still a nomad at heart and permanent structures were against the natural grain of his existence. Moreover, to the victorious Aryans, brick structures were symbolic of a people they had conquered and whose cities and towns they held in contempt.

As depicted in later carvings on stone and described in their great literary epics, the early Aryan village was a conglomerate of timber and thatch huts of different types (Fig.13). The most elementary of the huts was circular in plan, this being the simplest to construct with bamboo and thatch. The wall was made of upright bamboos tied together with twisted twigs. The roof made with bent bamboos took a domical or conical shape, made water-tight with over-lapping thatch or grass. Though easy to erect, the interior of a circular hut had obvious functional limitations. An addition was then made in

13. Variations of the timber, bamboo and thatch huts of the early Aryan village settlements of 1000 BC in the Ganges valley.

the form of a rectangular hut in front. In roofing this too the builders took advantage of the elastic nature of bamboo. Lengths of bamboos were bent into a semicircular shape and tied with a string at the base, much like the cord of a bow. A series of these put together over the two longer parallel bamboo walls of the hut created a barrel like roof, which again was covered with thatch and grass. The huts were arranged in groups of threes and fours around an open courtyard. A conglomerate of such units was the typical Aryan village.

13a. Timber and bamboo gateway installed along the village boundary wall the form of which was later transformed into the famous stone Toranas of the Buddhist

The village was defined and screened off from the wild life of the surrounding forest, by a timber fence. To erect it, rectangular wooden posts were planted at regular intervals. Three horizontal bamboo bars were then strung between the spaces by threading them into holes in the verticals, to complete the fence (Fig.13a). At points of entry a portion of the fence was projected out. A gateway was installed in front of it, constructed much like the fence with its horizontal ties raised high enough to provide a controlled entry through which cattle passed to and from the pasturage. Though these village structures were obviously of a temporary nature, the forms, shaped by the early Aryan carpenter, as we shall see, contained the embryo, of much of the later architecture of India, especially of the Hindu and Buddhist places of worship.

## RELIGION AND RITUAL OF THE ARYANS

The worship of images was not yet a part of Vedic religious ritual and no temples appear to have been constructed. The Vedic pantheon consisted rather of Devas—"The shining ones"—most of whom were personifications or symbols of natural phenomena like Dyaus-Pitra (Jupiter), the Sky father, Surya, Savitri or Mitra, the Sun God; Agni the sacred fire; and the most powerful and popular of them all, Indra, the ideal warrior. The central feature of Aryan religious life was the elaborate ritual of sacrifice to propitiate the Devas. The only architectural device required for such sacrifices was an open altar, the size and shape of which was determined by elaborate astronomical and mathematical calculations. Sacrifices on the altar could be conducted only by the learned poet-priest. He chanted hymns in classic Sanskrit in praise of the Devas, seeking their favours and goodwill for the ruling warrior aristocracy. In fact the famous Rig Veda is a book of 1028 such hymns collected together probably in 900 B.C. This monumental work is also the reason for this period of Indian history, between 600 and 120 B.C. being popularly referred to as the Vedic period.

## ADMINISTRATION AND ECONOMY

As the tribes settled down permanently in villages, they began to rapidly clear the forests for cultivation, by burning them down. Intensive agricultural activity on the clearings led to the concept of ownership of land, and the consequent emergence of a class of wealthy landlords who had sufficient capital and leisure to trade with the surplus produce of their lands. Since the cutting of roads through the animal infested dark jungles would have been a laborious task indeed, the rivers became the natural highways of this trade. Until now, the wars of the pastoral Aryan tribes had been fought over cattle, the accepted symbol of wealth. Now as agricultural economy and trade became more lucrative, the Aryan tribes began to war also for control of land as well as townships, that were developing to cater to the needs of trade. For reasons of security, individual tribes soon found it necessary to confederate into larger units to wage war. The civil administration of the Aryan village was left to 'Samitis' and 'Sabhas', analogous perhaps to a general body and an Executive Committee of today. The elected chief was supposed to be guided by the 'Sabhas'. Gradually, however, he began to assume the privilege of a king. In course of time, by 800 B.C. kingship was accorded a sense of divinity by the priests, a concept that worked to the mutual benefit of both the warrior and the emerging priestly class of Brahmins, who between the two controlled the reins of religious and temporal power.

## THE GREAT EPICS

The colourful religious, cultural and temporal life of this period is depicted in two epics, the Ramayana and the Mahabharata, in the form of legendary tales built probably around historic incidents and characters. The Ramayana describes the wandering of the legendary Prince Rama of Ayodhya who, with his wife Sita and brother Laxmana, is banished to the forests for 14 years, by a father who could not resist the machinations of Rama's step-mother. After many adventures with the ferocious aboriginal tribes of the south termed "Rakshasas", culminating in victory over the demon king Ravana of Lanka, Rama returns to his native Ayodhya. He is then crowned king and rules over an Utopian state. The other epic, Mahabharata, is renowned for being the longest single poem in the world. It revolves around the great struggle between the hundred brothers of the Kaurav tribe ruling from Hastinapur (near modern Ambala) and the five Pandavas with their capital at Indraprastha, most likely modern Delhi. The struggle culminates in victory for the Pandavas in the celebrated 18-day battle fought on the plains of Kurukshetra in modern Haryana. In the course of the battle, the legendary Lord Krishna delivers a message to a despondent warrior Arjuna, that contains the quintessence of the Aryan and later day Hindu philosophy of life in the form of the Bhagvada Gita.

## THE EMERGENCE OF TOWNS

The stories interwoven into the epics are evocative of the strife for power amongst the warring Aryan clans. Ultimately, by about 450 B.C. four rival states had maneuvered themselves into prominence—the three kingdoms of Kashi, Koshala and Magadha, and the Republic of the Virji's. The towns of these burgeoning kingdoms and republics, such as Shravasti, Champa, Rajgriha, Ayodhya, Kaushambi and Kashi had developed into centres of industry and trade. With the establishment of large urban settlements, architecturally speaking at least, India seemed to have reached a level of building and planning activity somewhat comparable to that of the Indus Valley civilization of over 1500 years ago.

14. The excavated remains of the ramparts of the 500 B C city of Kausambi, built with baked bricks of an immense size and rising to a height of over 9 metres.

15. Layout of an ideal vedic town and design of houses appropriate to the different castes as visualized by the Aryan town planners in their famous treatise, the Arthashastra.

Unlike the cities of Harappa and Mohenjodaro, the foundations of which were left intact once they had been deserted, most cities of the Gangetic plain have been continuously inhabited and constantly rebuilt. A number of the living cities even of today, are built over such ancient sites. Thus, the archaeologist excavating in the Gangetic plain has not been able to unearth the treasures that his predecessor in the Indus Valley had been able to. It is likely, however, that the ideal town of the period was meant to be laid out as a square with a gridiron pattern. Three main streets would run north-south and another three in the east-west direction as prescribed in the *Arthashastra*, the Indian manual of town planning compiled centuries later (Fig. 15 a, b, c).

Excavations at Kaushambi, near Allahabad, have revealed that this town was built largely with baked bricks of an immense size ($19'' \times 12\frac{1}{2}'' \times 2\frac{1}{2}''$) ($48 \times 30 \times 5$ cms) instead of timber. Houses were built around the traditional central open-to-sky-courts. The city was protected with ramparts over 30 feet (9 metres) high built in mud, revetted externally with a battered facing of big bricks (Fig.14). Rectangular towers were erected upon the bastions at varying intervals. Even the excavated site of today reveals an imposing facade. The town was also served by a rudimentary sewage system equipped with soak pits, made of superimposed jars with perforated bases. Archaeological evidence suggests that Kaushambi is typical of the north Indian town during the middle of the first millenium B.C. It would thus seem that by about 500 B.C. after over a thousand years of settlement in India, the Aryans had established a comfortable urban way of life in the plains of the Ganga in cities such as Kusingara (Fig.12).

# 3

# Buddha, Mahavira and the Mauryas

## The "Garden City" of Pataliputra

THE evolution of the Aryans' nomadic ways to urbane ways of life gave birth to a new elite class of merchants, artists' guilds and bureaucrats. To this materially progressive group residing in the towns and cities Vedic religion as instituted by the Brahmins was of a rather mechanical and lifeless character. It involved the performance of rituals and repugnant bloody sacrifices that were cumbersome to the busy city dweller. The prosperous urbanites, who had worked their way up the social ladder, also resented the fact that the professional priest, apart from having abrogated all religious merit and powers to himself, was reluctant to give up the place he had appropriated at the top of the gradually stratifying caste system. This conflict between established orthodoxy and the "aspirations of newly rising groups in the urban centres" led to the growth of religious and philosophical speculations that confronted the institutionalised hegemony of the Brahmins. Some groups of non-Brahmin ascetics, having acquired psychic powers through severe penance, challenged the Brahmin claim of attributing magical religious powers only to the ritual of sacrifices conducted by him. The supporters of the atheistic philosophy of Sankhya, on the other hand, recognized the dualism of "matter and soul" and preached that normalcy was merely the result of a balance of the three qualities of virtue, passion and dullness, the worship of the Brahmin pantheon of Gods having nothing to do with it. Sects, such as the Charvakas with no mean following, dared even to preach total materialism: "When the body dies, both fool and wise are alike cut off and perish."

### PRINCE SIDHARTHA OF THE SHAKYAS

It was in such an atmosphere of speculation, inquiry and defiance of the established order that Prince Sidhartha Gautam of the semi-royal Shakya tribe, renounced the pleasures and delights of a princely life that seemed to him artificial and in sharp contrast with the suffering and miseries of life outside the luxurious confines of his palace. Clad in hermit's robe he set out in search of a new path of peace and happiness. For several years Gautam studied the teachings of the Upanishads (commentaries on Vedas by various ancient sages), the techniques of meditation and even practised rigorous self-mortification. However, none of these showed him the way to the liberation of life from sorrow and suffering. Ultimately, after 49 days of continuous persevering meditation, in 528 B.C. when he was 35 years old, he found enlightenment. As

16. Of the once great timber and stone Mauryan palace of Pataliputra, nothing remains but the scanty foundations also built in timber.

Gautam the Buddha, he set the "wheel of law" rolling in his first sermon given at the Deer Park in Sarnath, near present day Varanasi. To the five disciples who heard this sermon, he preached that suffering is caused by human desire; emancipation is only possible through the eight-fold path of right views, resolve, speech, conduct, livelihood, effort, recollection and meditation. The sermon was simple and rational, not involved with complex metaphysical thinking, nor alluding to any abstract concept of God or requiring complicated rituals of worship. This became Buddha's "middle path" to *Nirvana*, or freedom from the eternal wheel of birth and rebirth. To a nation weary of the endless machinations of the Brahmins, Buddha's message was a welcome soothing balm. The "middle path", over the decades was to be adopted by millions of followers of the new religion of Buddhism, the world over.

Vardhamana, another scion of an oligarchic martial clan, had also much like Gautam set out and found his own path to salvation, 18 years earlier; his vision was to lead to the founding of another major Indian religion, that of Jainism. To Vardhamana, the Mahavira, the concept of God and the abstruse teachings of the Brahmins were of no value. "A soul resides in all things, material or otherwise." The aim of life is eternal bliss which is possible only by purification of the soul and could be achieved by living a balanced monastic life of which nonviolence was the touchstone.

## KINGSHIP IN THE NORTHERN PLAINS

The Buddhist and Jaina preaching of peace and nonviolence, however, had little effect on contemporary temporal life. Rulers of the city-kingdoms and republics continued to battle ferociously for control of strategic territories. With four major contenders in the fray, the battles now were, so to say, in the semi-final stages. The kingdom of Magadha, with its capital at Rajgriha, located in a valley surrounded by five hills, near modern Patna, was gradually emerging as the champion power. Ultimately India's first historically acknowledged king, Bimbisara, led the armies of Magadha to victory over the rulers of Kasi and Koshala. Bimbisara's son Ajatashatru aided by new weapons like stone-throwing catapults and chariots fixed with knives and cutting edges, finally defeated the armies of the Republic of the Virjis in 475 B.C. after a 16-year war. With this decisive victory, Ajatashatru firmly established the Aryan concept of kingship in the plains of the Ganga.

The monarchical system brought its own trail of court intrigues and jealousies. Ajatashatru, who himself had gained his kingdom by killing his father, was followed by a virtual dynasty of parracides. When the last of these was overthrown, nine Nanda kings followed each other in quick succession. Their 40-year rule from Magadha was never very popular. The authority of Mahanandid, the last of the Nandas, was challenged by Chandragupta, a young chieftain of the tribe of the Mauryas. Following the astute advice of his wily Brahmin counsellor, Vishnugupta,—also known to history as Chanakya and Kautilya,—Chandragupta bided his time. He chose to press towards the Indus region, avoiding an immediate confrontation with Mahanandid.

## CYRUS AND THE TRANS-INDUS REGION

The area west of the Indus, former home of the Indus Valley civilization that had been abandoned by the invading Aryans, had remained sequestered from the development of the Aryan tribal society of the Gangetic plain to a monarchial system. Cyrus, the great Persian emperor, had crossed the Hindukush mountains some 200 years earlier, and easily established sovereignty over the various disunited tribes of Kamboja, Gandhara, and other trans-Indus regions.

Taksashila or Taxila located in the present Haro Valley (near modern day Rawalpindi), the ancient capital of the Gandhara region had inevitably become the meeting point of Vedic and Persian learning. Though Taxila had little pretensions to being a city of great architecture, its scanty remains show that there was some semblance of planning (Fig. 17) in the layout of its

17. Plan of a portion of the 250 B C city of Taxila showing the haphazard growth in comparison to the well ordered cities of the Indus Valley civilisation. Left, an image of the Buddha.

main and subsidiary streets. The pebble walled and plastered houses in Taxila were much inferior to the brick and timber dwellings of Harappa and Mohenjodaro. This first city known to archaeologists as Sirkap (or the Bhirmound), was to rise to greater eminence when it was rehabilitated and rebuilt after the Greek invasion of India. In its present form it was only a living example of how the civic lessons of town planning of the Indus Valley civilization had been all but forgotten. It was at Sirkap, however, that the Persian craftsman, whose ancestors had built the great masonary palace of Darius I, and Xerxes, introduced the art of stone carving and polishing to his Indian contemporary. A most fortuitous event, indeed. As we shall see, it added an entirely new and momentous dimension to the building arts in India, which were for ever destined to be dominated by the craft of stone carving and sculpture.

## ALEXANDER, PORUS AND CHANDRAGUPTA

The Persians retained control over the trans-Indus region until their own empire crumbled under Greek pressure. After defeating Darius II in the famous battle of Marathon, Alexander's Greek armies appeared in the Indus Valley in 326 B.C. His famous campaign in India lasted from February until October, during which he crossed the five rivers of the Punjab. On the banks of the Beas, however, his army tired and exhausted after its long campaign and hard-won victory over the Indian King Porus, refused to go further. Though Alexander's ambitions were far from fulfilled, he was forced to relent and decided to return by following the course of the Indus down to the Arabian sea. In the process he left behind a floating Greek population, and a power vacuum in the entire region. Chandragupta, the Maurya, waiting patiently in the wings filled the vacuum admirably and was soon acknowledged leader of a confederation of northern Aryan tribes. In the meanwhile Chandragupta's greatest ally, the wily Chanakya, had conveniently created conditions of chaos and revolt in the kingdom of Magadha. It was an opportune time for the now powerful Chandragupta to return and evict the last Nanda king. Thus, early in the third century B.C. and for the first time in Indian history the plains of the two great Indian rivers, the Indus and the Ganga, came under a single great ruler—Chandragupta Maurya. Just as Ajatashatru some 150 years earlier had established the concept of Kingship in India, Chandragupta Maurya could easily lay claim to being the first Emperor of India.

Chandragupta ruled his empire with an iron hand for almost a quarter century with an efficiently structured army, police and bureaucracy. His Prime Minister and mentor, Chanakya, minutely describes all aspects of administering and maintaining a kingdom and its many burgeoning cities, in the now famous political treatise the "Arthashastra".

## THE MAURYAN CITY OF PATLIPUTRA

The Mauryan capital city of Patliputra (modern Patna) of 2000 years ago, stretched for nine miles along the Ganga being only one and half miles deep inland. The king's palace (Fig. 16) was most likely a grand version of the familiar rectangular hut of the humble village; a series of barrel-vaulted timber roofs supported over rows of stone columns instead of brick walls. The columns were crafted either by the immigrant Persian artisans of Taxila or Indian disciples trained in their workshops. Nothing, however, remains of these structures, except some finely jointed timber foundations excavated near modern Patna, our conjectures being based on the Buddhist craftsman's penchant for depicting scenes of Buddha's life against vivid backgrounds of the cities of the day.

According to Megasthanese, the famous Greek envoy to the capital city of the Mauryan empire, the King's palace was set within beautiful parks studded with lakes, fountains, sprays, swings and artificial hillocks. The entire complex was protected by a timber reinforced wall. The city itself was a cluster of houses of varying plans invariably covered with barrel-shaped roofs, waterproofed with tiles or thatch. These, as the sculptured friezes of Buddhist stone carvers depict, had horse-shoe shaped windows and lattice screened balconies overlooking the street. These must have presented a more exuberant and lively ensemble (Fig. 18) than that of the rather bleak and blank walled streets of Mohenjodaro and Harappa.

In the suburbs were the larger houses of the well-to-do, built around open courtyards, and surrounded by private gardens. Large public groves seem to have been laid out for the "recreation of man and beast." If Megasthanese's description of the towns of the Mauryan period is accurate, the town planning ideas of the time seem to be similar to that of the socalled 19th century "garden city" concept of Ebenezer Howard.

18. The Buddhist carvers depiction of the balconied and windowed streets of the Mauryan towns, that were so much more lively than the rather bleak windowless streets of Mohenjodaro.

# 4

# The Ahimsa of Asoka the Great

## The Stupa, the Stambha and the Vedika

CHANDRAGUPTA'S son Bimbisara, who succeeded to the throne in 297 B.C., extended the limits of the Mauryan empire as far south as modern Mysore. His son, the Great Asoka, came to power in 272 B.C., and for some time continued the ambitious policy of expansion with as much zeal as his father and grandfather. He laid siege to the neighbouring kingdom of Kalinga (modern Orissa). After the prolonged and now famous, savage war he was finally able to conquer the kingdom of Kalinga, eight years after his consecration as King. The hard earned victory over Kalinga, however, did not turn out to be a source of jubilation for Asoka. Rather, he seemed to have been greatly affected by the ensuing misery and suffering; a hundred and fifty thousand taken prisoner, a hundred thousand killed in war and many more rendered homeless and dead. This, as one of his inscriptions tells us "Asoka Priyadasi—the beloved of the gods—found very pitiful and grievous." Hereafter, King Asoka determined to atone for his sins by setting up an enlightened government and in due course of time even entertained ambitions of becoming the "moral leader of the whole civilized world".

The religion propagated by Gautama the Buddha was tailormade for Asoka's "moral ambitions". He adopted it wholeheartedly and vigorously set about the task of propagating the message of Buddha not only to the confines of the Indian subcontinent but the whole world. He supported the doctrine of Ahimsa (non-violence), substituted pilgrimages to Buddha's holy places for hunting expeditions, and even appointed so called "Officers-of Righteousness" to see that his humanitarian reforms were carried out. The first architectural manifestations of Asoka's campaign for Buddhism was to give the many nondescript earth and rubble structures, that housed the relics and ashes of the Buddha, a distinguished and durable form; in fact, to transform these wayside shrines into monuments in the glory of the Buddha.

## THE MONUMENTAL PRINCIPLES OF THE ANCIENT

Ancient monumental edifices all over the world have always been structured on the principle of being built over a wide base with the superstructure decreasing gradually in size towards an apex of sorts. To attain height, monumentality and structural stability, with essentially inelastic materials like

19. The Laurya Nandgarh lion sculpture proclaiming the "Dharma" to the Buddhist world of Asoka.

stone and brick, this was the soundest way of assuring a long life for the edifice. A solid monument of this nature creates virtually no lateral forces unlike, say, a cubic mass that would need to be contained within well reinforced and massive walls of mortar jointed masonry. Rather the load of the gradually tapering structure acts only downwards and as long the building material of the lowest course is not crushed by its own weight, structural immortality is virtually inherent in the design. The actual form that emerged from this sound principle, acquired various shapes in different regions, influenced as it was by local geographical, geological, climatic, social and religious reasons.

20. A Ziggarut of ancient Assyria.

It is also no wonder then that though the houses and palaces of ancient times have vanished, buildings like the pyramids of the Egyptian's, Aztecs and Assyrians and the stupas of the Buddhists are still extant. The builders of Egypt for their memorials had crystallized the shape of the familiar sand dunes of the desert into great pyramids (Fig. 23) or, may be, attempted to symbolise the rays of the sun from horizon to horizon, in its profile. The Assyrian cut stepped terraces into the sides of the pyramid to create the famous Ziggaruts (Fig. 20) more suited probably to the performance of their sacred rituals. Even in far away Mexico, the Aztecs built their temples, over piles of receding masonry, designed virtually like monumental staircases to the heavens above (Fig. 21). The one structural principle common to the Egyptian, the Assyrian and Aztec builder though is, that he always started from a broad base tapering to a narrow apex. Just as the ancient craftsman the world over had built his monumental edifices over a plan that was an elementary geometric profile, the evident choice open to the Buddhist architect was either a square or a circle, the two purest and most perfect of geometric forms. He chose the circle; to him not only did it symbolise the Buddhist "wheel of law" but was also an ideal focus for performing the Buddhist ritual of endless circumambulation

21. A Mexican Pyramid with "staircases to the heavens".

of a sacred object. Moreover, its connotations were significantly contrary to the square which had formed the basis of the plans of the Vedic altars of sacrifice.

## THE BUDDHIST STUPA

And so the irregular humble mound of rubble that had been piled over by the reverent worshippers over relics, and ancient treasures to mark a sacred site, was now transformed by the royal builders into a hemispherical brick paved tumulii, the plan, elevation, section and total form of which were all derived from the circle (Fig. 22). The embryo of the most powerful architectural form of Buddhism, the famous Stupa, thus emerged for the first time under the architectural patronage of Asoka.

Asoka, however, seems to have been fully aware of the transitory nature of such mud and brick stupas, however elaborately decorated. Since his proclaimed aim was to ensure a "long endurance of the good law," he inevitably started "thinking in stone." In his meticulously planned operation, not unlike a modern advertising campaign for the spread of Buddhism, he was quick to use the well tried techniques of the Persian emperor Darius. Messages of Buddha, in the Pali text, were carved into tablets of stone and installed at various strategic locations (Fig. 24). The success of his campaign can be gauged by the fact that a number of these effectively affirm the gospel of the Buddha to his followers as much as 2,000 years after they were erected.

22. A circle in plan, a circle in elevation, the essence of the Buddhist stupa.

23. The great pyramids of the ancient Egyptians at Gizeh near modern Cairo.

# THE STAMBHAS

To these stele's Asoka also added his own special innovation. Inspired undoubtedly by the wooden totem poles of the primitive tribes, he ordered the inscriptions carved on columns of stone instead of mere slabs and these were set up at regular intervals along roads leading to places of Buddhist pilgrimage. The Indian stone mason had learnt his lesson well from the Persian "gurus." In what may be called his first test in the crafting of stone, he carried out the emperor's commands with great sculptural and technological ingenuity. Columns, some 40 feet (12 metres) in length and weighing as much as 50 tonnes, were carved out from a single block of sandstone, won out of the now famous quarry at Chunnar, in modern Bihar. These massive pillars were then carried, unbroken and intact to sites over hundreds of miles away. The means of transport employed for this amazing feat are still not clear. Presumably, the operation involved building specially designed, huge bullock-drawn timber carts, and even flat barges (Fig. 25) for floating down the well tried highways of trade—the numerous Indian rivers.

24. An Asokan stone-edict.

25. The "single piece" 50 ton stambhas were transported across the Indian countryside on timber carts and floated on the rivers in huge flat barges.

The tapering shaft of the column, once it had reached its destination, was painstakingly varnished and polished to give it a unique and unbelievable mirror-like lustre; a fantastic achievement indeed, with a sedimentary rock like sandstone. The column, it would appear, sometimes rose straight out of the ground without any base, like the trunk of a tree, or at some places had a circular brick platform at its base. At the top was mounted a large sculptured figure of an animal.

26. The famous Buddhist sculpture of the four lions from Sarnath.

One of these, the famous sculpture of the *four-lions* (Fig. 26) has acquired great popularity since being adopted as the national emblem of modern India. The sculpture executed in a style reminiscent of Persian design, weighing five tonnes and about seven feet in height, was effectively joined to the pillar by a 2 feet (60 cm.) long cylindrical copper dowel, toned accurately into the shaft and sculpture without use of any cementing material. A magnificent, large as life lion sitting high in the air (as at Lauriya Nandgarh in Bihar) (Fig. 19) proclaiming the *dharma* to the world, must indeed have been a wonderous sight to the Buddhist pilgrims of the second century B.C.

## THE AJIVIKAS AND CAVE ARCHITECTURE

Though Asoka zealously propagated Buddhism virtually as the state religion, he was not entirely intolerant of other sects. The Ajivika ascetics were another of his beneficiaries. He ordered sancturies, to suit their needs, to be built at the cost of the state. As if to prove the basic tenets of their thinking, that "all change and movement were illusionary" and the "world in reality was eternally and immovably at rest" the Ajivikas discarded the conventional timber and brick structures of the materially engrossed oppidian. They chose instead to carve out habitable caves out of the "eternally immovable" hill sides, for their sanctuaries. Also in chosing this novel form of architecture, they intuitively immortalized the traditional dwelling of the Indian sage, who as a mark of the rebellion from the materialistic creed of the city dweller, had for years sought refuge to meditate in natural caves in eremitical hillsides. Unknowingly, the Ajivikas had pioneered an art form, that was to flower into some of the most unique works of Indian architecture.

27. The Lomas Rishi carved out by the Ajivikas in 250 B C was the first step towards the creation of the great art of cave architecture of the Buddhists.

In the shaping of these caves, the builders with chisels and hammers as their main tools, were practising more the craft of sculpture than of architecture. They were unhindered by the bother of calculating spans, adequate supports and checking the strength of materials. If they had really chosen to exercise their freedom and thrown to the wind all the normal restraints of traditional building forms, they could well have produced a hundred bizzare and exotic shapes. However, an inherent love, or weakness if you will, for the familiar, made them reproduce in rock, almost exact copies of existing structures in wood and thatch.

This curious and novel adaptation of the carpenter's art to the stone carvers, however, produced its own inimitable results, that can be seen in some seven caves of the Ajivikas in the hills of Barabar and nearby Nagrajuni, north of modern Bhubaneswar in Orissa. Of these, the cave popularly known as Lomas Rishi is surely the crowning glory. Its interior circular cell 19 feet (6 metres) in diameter has a hemispherical domed roof and is approached through a 33 feet (10 metres) long tunnel-like hall (Fig. 28). The barrel-vaulted rectangular thatch hut and the beehive roofed shrine, crafted by the Aryan carpenter and to be found in any of the innumerable Indian villages, had thus been perpetuated in the form of a cave. The shape of the entrance arch on the hill-side is the familiar gable, end of the same rural-dwelling, described earlier (Fig. 27). The minutest structural details of the original hut have been faithfully reproduced in the Lomas Rishi. The rockcutters however lifted this work beyond mere plagiarism by deftly introducing a beautifully sculptured semi-circular panel at the crown of the arch depicting two rows of elephants walking towards a stupa. Such a panel could neither have been lifted nor inspired by any timber structure; only a skilled stone carver could have conceived of it and created it (Fig. 29). This combination of traditional building forms and applied sculpture obviously appealed immensely to the flowering genius of the Indian artist. It became, as we shall see, the unique essence of all Buddhist and Hindu architecture in India, for centuries to come.

During and for a considerable time after Asoka's death in B.C. 232, well up to the end of the Mauryan dynasty, Buddhism for all purposes enjoyed the status of a state religion. The third Great Council of Buddhism was held in Pataliputra, under the patronage of Asoka, to iron out the widespread differences between the various ever-proliferating orders of Buddhist monks. Buddha may have propounded only a doctrine to help

28. Caves fashioned in plan, elevation and section to resemble thatch and timber huts of the Aryan village.

29. One of the earliest sculptural embellishments applied by stone carvers to caves inspired by the traditional timber forms—the entrance to the Lomas Rishi cave.

his followers on the path to salvation. His teachings, however, had generated a large international following—a following so large that it evolved into one of the earliest established religions of the world. In the country of its birth, however, it was at loggerheads with the contemporary thinking of the Brahmins, Jains and Ajivikas.

## THE CULT OF THE CHAITYAS

In the process of maturing into a religion, Buddism borrowed little from the sacrificial rites of the Brahmins; rather its simple ritual was inspired by the popular cult of the "Chaityas" (from the Sanskrit *chita*—a pyre) or "sacred spots". The traditional chaitya was a grove of trees in the middle of which small tumulii of earth had been built up over the ashes of the tribal chiefs. The rural folk found these chaityas, located on the outskirts of their villages, less expensive and more convenient to worship than the great Aryan gods. The Buddhist monks merely transferred the attention of their followers, from these to stupas that carried in them, ashes or relics of the Buddha.

With the growth of a large lay following and the assured patronage of the elite and rich mercantile classes, communities of Buddhist monks, instead of wandering around as alm begging mendicants, began settling down around such chaityas. The chaityas thus grew into small monasteries and the cult of the chaitya became the touchstone of Buddhist ritual and worship. By the time of Asoka's death, the Indian countryside was probably dotted by a number of such Buddhist settlements.

These establishments, to begin with, were of a very modest nature, much like the wayside village shrine of today. The stupa at best was a white-washed mound, probably decorated with festoons and prayer flags. A protective wooden fence around the stupa, apart from symbolising the sacred nature of the enclosed area, demarcated a circumambulatory path along which monks would walk around the stupa, chanting Buddhist "slokas" or holy scriptures. Near the stupa were probably some simple thatch huts for the resident monks. By the very temporary nature of their construction, none of these settlements have survived to this date. Curiously enough, the more permanent and enduring architectural masterpieces of the Buddhists were destined to be constructed after the patronising umbrella of the Mauryan dynasty vanished.

# 5

# The Shungas, the Merchants and the Buddhists

## "Heavenly domes" of Sanchi

THE long reign of Asoka was undoubtedly a benevolent one. Nevertheless it was an autocracy, even if a religious one, or more precisely a Buddhist one. Brahmin discontent had been constantly simmering beneath the tight administrative organization of a centralized Mauryan authority. Gradually, the pivot of this authority had become the figure of emperor Asoka himself. Not surprising, then, that the power of the great Mauryan dynasty was swiftly eroded by repeated rebellions of the malcontent Brahmins, within fifty years of the death of Asoka. The spearhead of this rebellion was Pushyamitra, a Brahmin of Kanauj in central India, and a General in the army, who murdered the last Mauryan king and heralded the dynasty of the Shungas in 185 B.C. The Shunga kings, for some unknown curious reason, did not take any regal title but were content to style themselves as "Senapati" or General. This dynasty of Generals with its warlike postures paid little heed to the peaceful messages of the Buddhist religion. Inevitably with the revival of the rule of Brahmins and their Kshatriya commanders, the Aryan rites of Vedic sacrifice were once again popularly patronized. The elaborate Ashvamedha Yagna, whereby an Aryan chief not only proclaimed suzerainty over a tract of territory but threw a gauntlet at any other contender, was performed by the Shungas, signalling the return of true orthodox Brahminism to the land of its birth.

### THE GROWTH OF SANCHI

In such an intimidating atmosphere, the orders of Buddhist monks began to retire from the centres of urban power. They however, continued to enjoy the patronage of the wealthy and sophisticated mercantile class that had little to gain by servility to the rising powers of resurgent Brahminism, since their place in society was virtually preordained. Funds continued to pour in to help the order of Buddhist monks to build their new monasteries in more peaceful and solitary environments. The largest and most famous of these blossomed upon a hill top in Sanchi (near modern Bhopal) close to Vidisha, the new centre of Shunga power (Fig.31). Sanchi had already been marked as a sacred spot when a semi-circular brick mound some 70 feet (21.3 metres) in diameter had been built here, as a part of Asoka's historic architectural campaign. The stupa was now enlarged to double its size (Fig. 30) by building another stone-faced mound, increasing the diameter of the original to 120 feet (36.5 metres) and its height to 54 feet

30. The largest "heavenly dome" at Sanchi which has a diameter of 36.5 metre and rises to a height of more than 16 metres.

31. Plan of excavated ruins and structures of the Buddhist monastery at Sanchi.

37

(16.4 metres). Sixteen feet high from the ground level of the Stupa the builders created an elevated Pradakshina Path perhaps reserved for the clergy, the traditional one at ground level being open to the common pilgrim. The crown of the hemispherical mound was flattened out to make place for a circular platform, from the middle of which rose a three tiered stone umbrella, set inside a square enclosure, marked out by a low stone fence.

## THE STONE VEDIKA

In the process of carrying out the enlargement of the stupa, the traditional timber fence surrounding the original stupa had to be pulled down. It was now replaced by a massive and austere railing, fabricated entirely out of stone (Fig. 32). In assembling together this railing the craftsmen of India were taking yet another decisive step towards the proficient use of stone as a comprehensive building medium. They were already pastmasters in the sculpting and polishing of stone and had successfully installed massive Asokan pillars all over India. Now the masons, though diffident, were ready to carry out their first experiment in the use of stone as a semistructive material. No wonder then that they went about their task in a truly ponderous fashion. Octagonal stone pillars 18 inch (45 cm) in diameter and 9 feet (2.7 metres) high were planted along the circular periphery at a distance of about 2 feet (60 cm) from each other. The space between each pair was spanned by three, 2 feet (60 cm) deep, lens-shaped horizontals, which were meticulously tenoned into corresponding mortices cut in the pillars (Fig.33). The railing was topped by an appro-

**32 & 33.** Ponderous octagonal stone pillars were planted close together and spanned with lens shaped horizontals to replace the original impermanent timber vedika around the stupa.

priately massive stone coping, giving it a total height of 11 feet (3.3 metres). It is obvious that the shape and form of the security oriented timber fence around the Aryan village, a prototype of which had surrounded the early Buddhist stupa, had over the centuries also acquired sacred and magical virtues. Thus, in the entire process of erecting the sacrosanct Vedika in stone, the craftsman had diligently reapplied the structural techniques of the Aryan carpenter so as not to tamper with the physiognomy of the timber original. Constructed to a different scale and infused with the tenacious vitality of the new material of hewn rock, this railing alone created an awesome wonder (Fig. 34). The raw visual power of its architectonics is no less than that of the primitive megaliths of Stonehenge in England and Zimbabwe in Rhodesia.

34. Transformed into rock, the original fragile timber vedika suddenly acquired the awesome and wonderous qualities of Stonehenge and Zimbabwe.

## THE BUDDHIST TORANA

The work on the extensions and refurbishing of the stupa went on for almost a 100 years. The imagination, religious zeal and vigour of the builder as well as the coffers of the mercantile patronage, however, seemed inexhaustible. The designers were soon devising schemes to add new dimensions to the architectural ensemble. The wonderous pathway around the stupa was like a forbidding wall from outside. A touch of invitation was lacking. What more appropriate than to install gateways (Fig.35) to match the magnificence of the Vedika. Elaborating once again on traditional village forms, the rural bamboo gateway of the Aryan village was transformed by the Buddhist builders into a great 34 feet (10.3 metres) high Toran (from Sanskrit *Tor*—a pass). Four such gateways were installed at cardinal points of the railing. The techniques of stone masonry employed in constructing the toranas were no doubt as primitive as those in erecting the railing. Nevertheless, after erecting the two stone uprights the stone mason realised the futility of cutting mortices and making tenons in stone. Instead for the first time, he applied the rationale of building with stone and merely spanned the twenty feet between the verticals with curved stone beams resting firm and square and sailing over on either side of the uprights (Fig. 36). The horizontal spaces beween the beams were then filled in with vertical uprights to create a sort of stone trellis, the "jharokas" of which were adorned with sculpture. The surfaces of the two pillars as well as the cross beams along the top received a generous measure of the carvers chisel and were covered with finely wrought sculpture, rich in the symbolism and imagery of Buddhist lore. It is in fact the sensuous sculpture on these gateways that has provided the Indian historian with an invaluable visual record of the myths, legends and social mores of the day.

35. The stupa, surrounded by vedika with gateways at the four cardinal points.

36. The timber gate of the Aryans was transformed by the Buddhists into ceremonial gateways for their stupas, its surfaces bearing lively depictions of Buddhist legends.

# SYMBOLISM AND STRUCTURAL FUNCTION

The final tectonic composition comprising the dome of the Stupa (or the *Anda*) the square railing at the crown (or the *Harmika*) and the three tier umbrella (or *chatra*) have in course of time been invested with various elaborate geomantic, theological and philosophical meanings. The hemisphere is the "Dome of Heaven" or "the fixed cosmic structure", the Harmika "Heaven of the 33 gods," the umbrella "the world axis". The plan of the pradakshina-path at the ground level is read to be a *Swastika* and pregnant with the symbolism of ancient solar cults. The structural reasons for the development of such forms are however, much more pertinent. The hemispherical stupa, as explained earlier, was a geometric crystallization of the rudimentary mound of earth eminently suitable for the ritual of endless circumambulation (Fig. 37). The Harmika and chatra, are a stylised visual depiction of the famous Bodhi tree surrounded by the sacred Vedika—or railing. The Swastika is most likely the fortuitous result of solving a planning problem. The torana, erected after the railing was completed, was planted some feet away from the railing. The location of its entrance was staggered from the opening in the railings, so as to ensure privacy for the pilgrim circumbulating the Pradkshina (Fig.38), a planning principle, effectively employed later in the entrance gateways to fortresses for ensuring security. Seen purely in plan, the metaphysical observer would of course read the Swastika in its ensuing outlines.

38. A staggered gateway to ensure privacy for the pradakshina path or to intentionally chalk out the sacred Swastika in plan?

37. What started as a pile of rubble over sacred remains, was gradually crystallized into the spherical stupa.

## THE BUDDHIST VIHARA

An ensemble as glorious as the great stupa inevitably led to the growth of other ancillaries. Buildings were needed to house the resident monks. In contrast to the richly sculptured gateways of the stupas, the places of residence in their bareness, reflect rather the inherent austerity of monastic life. These were built as a series of individual cells or dormitories enclosing a rectangular or square open-to-sky court. The open court served all the community facilities, at places including a well for drinking water (Fig. 39). The cells, on the other hand, afforded the monks sufficient privacy for the practice of meditation. As one can see the basic idea was only an enlargement of the traditional concept of the "house around a courtyard" harking back to the days of the Indus Valley civilization. In due course, these came to be known as "Viharas". Since they were built in one or more stories, in timber frame and brick walls, only the foundations of these at Sanchi have survived the superstructure having vanished soon after the monasteries were deserted.

39. Remains of one of the many courtyard vihara's that provided residence for the Buddhist monks of Sanchi.

# CHAITYA HALLS

The great stupa, though a magnificent structure, had its limitations. It was essentially an open air edifice incapable of being used in inclement weather. The need was felt, therefore, for an enclosed hall in which a miniature stupa (so far the only acceptable symbol of Buddhist veneration) could be conveniently worshipped the year round. The simplest solution was to place the stupa at the end of a long rectangular hall (Fig. 40). Soon, however, the designers realised that the circular stupa sat rather incongruously within its rectangular enclosure. The walls directly behind the stupa were then made semicircular to echo the profile of the stupa (Fig. 41).

**40, 41 & 42.** A makeshift rectangular hall for the stupa, duly transformed into an apsidal hall to echo the circular stupa and ultimately roofed over with a barrel vaulted and tiled roof to create the earliest permanent Chaitya halls.

The path for the ritual of circumambulation around the stupa was also thus clearly defined. The roof of such a structure was the familiar barrel vault in timber, covered with tile and supported on brick walls framed by timber pillars. The entire composition was built on a high plinth enclosed by the inevitable sacred railing. The nascent form of the famous apsidal ended halls of worship, essentially like Roman basicilicas in plan, thus emerged in the so called Temple No.40 of Sanchi; (Fig. 42) a form that was to captivate the obsessions of the Buddhist builder, though in another medium, and result in the famous Chaitya caves at Ajanta, Ellora and Karle.

43. The monastery of Sanchi as it must have been in its heyday almost 2000 years ago.

A congregation of such chaitya halls, viharas, votive stupas and the inevitable Asoka pillars, dispersed on terraces at various levels around the great white stupa on the hill of Sanchi (Fig. 43) must have been an awe-inspiring sight to Buddhist pilgrims, about the time of the birth of Christ. For the Buddhist architect and craftsman, it represented a century of building endeavour, during which he had evolved the essential principles of design of forms that were destined to be the eternal architectural symbols of the religion of Buddha; the vihara, the chaitya, the vedika, the stambha and the stupa. These, as we shall see, were elaborated upon for hundreds of years by craftsmen not only in distant parts of India, but in the various nations that adopted Buddha's "middle path" as their way to salvation.

# 6

## The Andhras of the South

### Stupa of Amravati and caves of Karli

WHILE Buddhist monasteries like Sanchi flourished under the ever benevolent mercantile umbrella, the Shunga Kings were hard-pressed to preserve the empire bequeathed to them by the Mauryans. As early as 206 B.C. the Selucid Greeks had exposed the chinks in the defence of the north-west borders of the Mauryan empire by defeating the Indian King Subhagsena. Now Menandaer, a Bactrian Greek King having thrown off the Selucid yoke, controlled the entire western region of Sindh and Punjab and made raids deep in the Ganges valley, right up to the former Mauryan capital of Magadha. The Shungas were also being harassed from the east by the Kalinga King Kharavela, who, though professing to be a follower of the Jaina religion, was as war-like as any. Kharavela had once even captured Magadha in about 50 B.C. From the ruins of the southern empire of the Mauryans had risen the Satavahanas or the Andhras. From their capital city of Praisthana (modern Paithana) in the Deccan, they were constantly attacking the Shungas. Ultimately in 28 B.C., after ruling for almost a century, the Shungas capitulated to their nominal successors, the Kanvas. The Kanvas in turn were completely overrun by the Andhras, who about the turn of century, emerged as the ruling power, at least in southern and central India. It would seem that this turmoil and struggle for temporal power amongst the former vassals of the Mauryans, did not disturb the peace of the establishments of the various orders of the Buddhist monks. They continued to build and expand their great stupas and monasteries with unabated vigour.

### HOLLOW CORE STUPAS ON THE KISTNA AND THE GODAVARY

The monument that seems to have caught the fancy of the southern Buddhist builder, was the stupa. Numerous examples of this craft once dotted the countryside around the deltas of the Kistna and the Godavary rivers, the remains of more than ten sites having already been discovered. Unlike those at Sanchi, most of the stupas of the south were not enlargements of existing mounds; rather the entire hemispherical mound was often built up abinitio. While some of the earlier examples such as those at Bhattiprolu and Gudiada were built over a solid core of brick, the builders soon learnt to scientifically economise on the use of their giant size kiln burnt bricks, measuring as much as 24" × 18" × 4" (60 cm × 45 cm ×

44. The double height anteroom of the Bedsa cave in Western India, bathed in early morning light.

10 cm). Thus the core of a stupa at Ghantsala (Fig. 45) was formed by an inner circular core of brick walls radiating out much like the spokes of a wheel from the inner hub to the outermost circumference. These cross walls formed sectorial compartments which were filled with earth and rubble. This economy in construction, however, seems to have been more than amply made up by the lavish use of marble as a casing material at least for the lower drum, instead of the more austere yellow sandstone of Sanchi. The most sumptuous of this series of southern stupas would seem to be the one at Amravati, on the southern banks of the Kistna river.

## THE MARBLE STUPA OF AMRAVATI

Today nothing remains of the grand white mound of Amravati except an irregular trench marking its site. The very reasons for its great splendour seem to have hastened its desecration; its rich casing of marble made it a target of incessant vandalism. The few surviving marble slabs of its covering are now to be found only in museums in Madras, Calcutta and London.

45. Plan and section of the economically structured stupa of Ghantasala, with cross brick masonry walls to contain the earth filling.

46. A bas relief panel from the marble casing of the devastated Amaravati stupa of 300 A D.

47. Aryakas instead of Toranas to mark the cardinal entrance points of the Amaravati stupa.

Fortunately with the Buddhist builders "it was the practice to include in the carved decorations of the stupa small duplicate copies of itself in bar relief showing clearly and in full detail exactly what the main structure was like." From such panels (Fig. 46) and the existing remains, it is possible to infer that the Amravati stupa was about 190 feet (57.9 metres) in outer circumference, making it the largest stupa ever built in India. It was also the most profusely decorated, both architecturally and sculpturally. The cardinal points of the upper pradakshina path were marked out by clusters of free standing pillars or "Aryakas" giving an unusual artistic distinction to this southern type (Fig. 47). While no toranas seem to have been erected, the entrance to the lower pradakshina path are marked out by stambhas, which were also planted at regular intervals along the circumambulatory path. In structuring balustrades for the two "paths" the builders chose solid decorated marble panels for the upper one, while the lower one is a richly sculptured version of the traditional "vedika" of Sanchi.

Centuries ago, the great white marble stupa of Amravati must have been a dazzling monument to the glory of the great "Lord Buddha" who was now beginning to be worshipped as humane God and Saviour, rather than the mere propounder of a "middle path" to salvation.

49

In the meanwhile, Satkarni, the first great Andhra king, became an ardent supporter of the Brahmin faith and proclaimed his religious inclinations by performing the Ashwamedha Yagna of horse sacrifice. In spite of being able to carry out extensive building projects in the plains of the south and unhindered by actual persecution by the Andhras, the Buddhist seems to have read the writing on the wall. They were on the look-out for more isolated, secure and ermetic sites to build their monasteries. Their search led them to the so called ghats, where the Deccan Plateau falls down to the western coast in wild gorges and cliffs. They sensed that the uncertainties and turmoils of temporal power could not possibly penetrate into the virtually inaccessible forested hill sides. At the same time, trade routes, leading to the river port of Kalyan, ran parallel to the foot of the ghats and mercantile patronage would continue to be available.

## CAVES IN THE WESTERN GHATS

Until the arrival of the Buddhists there had been little building activity of any consequence in this difficult region. During their very first season in the hills in thatch huts, the monks must have had to face the fury of the rains. Rains which lashed down the hill side, virtually non-stop, for half the year, rains that could wash away an entire village without leaving a sign, and rains that would make worship around a stupa in the open an unpleasant task indeed. Under the circumstances, they could have ventured to build halls of worship, like the one at Sanchi. Timber was at hand from the forest. Bricks baked in the plains could, though with great difficulty, be hoisted up the steep hillsides. However, even such a hall, if successfully completed, would be difficult to maintain and preserve under the unrelenting fury of the monsoons. The hills alone, it would seem, could stand up to ravages of the incessant rains. With their great desire to make the Good Law of the Buddha outlast time itself, the Buddhist monks, taking a cue perhaps from the Ajivikas of Asoka's time, decided to carve their great sanctuaries out of the living rock of the immovable mountains.

They started with a few simple caverns, presumably to serve as a kind of site office for the "resident architect" or "clerk-of-works." The earliest known of these is at Bhaja. This experimental cutting gave rock carvers a working knowledge of the amygadaloid and cognate trap formations that made up the vertical bluffs of the ghats. The formations, being

**48.** The intricate stone carved details of timber joinery in the caves of Western India, were inspired by timber prototype Chaitya halls, constructed with a framework of timber with panels of brick.

of considerable thickness and marked uniformity, were found eminently suitable for the project in hand.

In carving out their great halls of worship at Bhaja they have reproduced as far as possible, an exact copy of existing structural chaitya halls, on a much grander scale (Fig. 48). Their dependance on traditional building forms as models for their caves, should not surprise us. Their Persian "gurus" 500 years earlier, in giving a facade to the rock-cut tomb of Darius at Nawsh-e-Rustom, had reproduced in toto, the elevation of a conventional built up Persepolis palace. Closer home, the Ajivikas in carving their caves at Barabar, had successfully done the same.

49. Facade of the 150 B C cave at Bhaja showing timber details incorporated into a stone facade.

## TECHNIQUES OF CAVE ARCHITECTURE

The intention of the monks then was to create the familiar apsidal ended chaitya hall in the living rock. The rock carvers got down to the technical details. The chosen hillside was cleared of shrubs and other growth. Having made it roughly vertical, the gable-end elevation of the structural chaitya hall, was sketched on the face of the rock wall. Two parallel tunnels were then run to the desired depth and timber wedges driven vertically into the exposed rock at convenient centres. When moistened, these wedges expanded and dislodged large chunks of stone, that were removed through the mouth of the cave. Once exposed, the desired surface of the rock was chiselled to final smoothness before breaking further downwards to avoid the tedious and expensive process of erecting a scaffolding later, to carry out polishing operations. Gradually with mere 1/4" (6 mm) chisels and hammers as the only tools, the excavation was carried on from the ceiling downwards. The entire volume of the hall with a fascimile of all the timber details of the structural chaitya on the inner surfaces, even down to the transverse rafters in the barrel-vault, was patiently won out of the living rock (Fig. 49).

The sides of the central arched opening in the face of the cliff were now decorated with living rock mock-ups of timber loggias and balconies. Finally, the ever dependable carpenters were then called in to cover up the large horse-shoe opening with a screen of timber trellis work, imitating the familiar sun window that was traditionally installed in structural chaitya halls (Fig. 50).

50. Sketch showing relationship of the rock facades, the intricate carving on it and the long cave cut into the living rock of the hill side.

The Buddhist clergy must have been immensly pleased with the outcome of their architects, sculptors and carpenters efforts at their very inception. Hereafter at various appropriate sites within a radius of about 100 miles numerous such chaitya halls were excavated. Some of the halls, at the now famous site of Ajanta (described later) are also a part of this early Buddhist movement.

The concept of recreating original timber structures in stone remained the essence of this movement. Gradually, however, the stone carver began to exploit the potential of the unique traits of his own art of rock cutting. Free as he was from the structural restraints of conventional building with great flamboyance he carved out barrel vaulted halls after halls each larger than its predecessor and more voluminous than any built so far with timber and masonry. The micro carvers and painters were not far behind the macro cutter. Columns that were plain shafts in the earliest examples, were enriched with sculptures and even paintings in later efforts. The chaitya arch under the growing confidence of the stone moulder took on various fanciful and fluid sculptural forms derived from rich Buddhist imagery, particularly that of the Lotus flower (Fig. 51). Timber trellis work on the facade was reduced to the minimum to ensure permanency. The monumental culmination of this peculiar art form, that for lack of adequate nomenclature has "been termed rock-cut architecture," is the famous mammoth hall at Karli, carved out of the western ghats, sometime in the first century A.D.

**51.** The fluid and graceful outlines of bamboo and timber forms were immortalized into window openings for the dark caves.

**52.** The Karle entrance was not merely an opening in the cliffside, but included a stately platform adorned with stambhas with lion sculptures.

53. Plan and section of the great Karle cave (100 B C) in the Western Ghats of India.

## KARLI, THE CAVE MAGNIFICENT

In plan this gigantic hall (45×150 ft) (14×46 metres) is not remarkably different from the others (Fig., 53). The designer of this cave was fully conscious of the potential of the visual drama and awe that could be infused into a visitor entering such a vast sacred hall. There were no mean staircases and ledges in the hillside to reach this chaitya. With the debris removed from the cave, a large artificial platform was built over the sloping hill side in front. The pilgrim on the platform is left ineffable by two enormous 50 feet (15.2 metres) high, free standing masonry columns crowned by glorious lion sculptures, standing like immovable sentinels on either side (Fig. 52). The facade behind is a rock-cut, two storey screen of stately columns. One passes into a double height ante-room or vestibule and is confronted by the recessed sun window set in a towering horse-shoe archway (Fig. 44). The walls are richly sculptured and the flat bare surfaces were at one time painted with colourful scenes from Buddha's legendary life. Through this magnificent facade, one enters the twilight space of the interior and gradually discerns the arrangement of a central apse flanked by massive columns, with two narrower ones on either side (Fig. 54). At the end of the deep cave looms the most sacred object of veneration, a sculpture of the Buddha moulded into the hemispherical profiles of the familiar stupa. The whole concept, execution and achievement of the indefinable space could only be the work of a thaumaturgist. Magic is created by soft effulgent luminosity rather than light, that filters in through the outer colonade, screens and the oriels of the sun window and falls like a delicate mantle on the stupa, situated seemingly, at the end of a fathom-less cavern. It is impossible not to be moved by the solemn majesty of this unique place of worship.

Builders were to return and continue to carve out cave after cave through the centuries at other sites, including the well known ones at Ajanta and Ellora. The latter builders however laid greater emphasis on the decorative rather than the spatial aspect. The chaitya hall of the first century A.D. at Karli remained, architecturally at least, an unrivalled wonder of the rock-cutters' art, and an unending source of inspiration to the Indian builder. For, as we shall see, though structural techniques evolved over the centuries, the Indian craftsman remained for ever conscious of the fragile and yet powerful relationship between light, space and sculpture that had endowed the caves of the Buddhists with magical qualities beyond the comprehensions of day to day architecture.

54. The magic quality of the space light and sculpture in the cave architecture of Buddhist India is something that has to be felt rather than merely seen. At Karli it is impossible not be moved by the "solemn majesty of this unique place of worship.

# 7

## The Greeks, Kushans and the "Larger Vehicle"

### The guilded shrines of Gandhara

WHILE Buddhist monks in western India had sought refuge from the vicissitudes of the unending feudal wars in secluded inaccessible sites, those in the north continued to play an active role in the rapidly changing political situation of the trans-Indus Gandhara region. Greek King, Menander, who had earlier made raids into central India, gained firm control over the region of the Punjab and Sindh and ruled over them from his capital at Sagala (modern Sialkot).

The city of Sagala has been described by a contemporary chronicler in stock glowing terms as "laid out by wise architects, with many and various strong towers and ramparts, splendid with hundreds of thousands of magnificent mansions and bazaars which face all quarters of the sky." Today, there is no trace of the towers, the mansions, or bazaars. During the its hey-day, the Buddhist monk, Nagasena, visited the capital with his disciples "lighting up the city with their yellow robes like lamps." Nagasena had acquired reputation and fame enough to prompt King Menander to go out and receive him personally, accompanied by his retinue of royal courtiers. There followed a catechismal discussion with Menander—the famous "Questions of Milinda"—that is said to have resulted in the King being converted to Buddhism.

In order to win such disciples, preachers of Buddhism were beginning to enlarge the scope of the simple doctrine preached by its founder. Buddha was accepted by Nagasena as "God" and "Saviour" and his graven image was now wor-

55. A carven image of a Buddha in the Gandhara style marking the acceptance of Buddha as "God and Saviour". Left the Takhte-Bahi monastery near modern Peshawar.

shipped as a deity (Fig.55). This interpretation of Buddhism became known as the *Mahayana* or larger vehicle while Buddha's original doctrine was designated as *Hinayana* or smaller vehicle.

## FUSION OF ROMAN, GREEK AND INDIAN STYLES

With the assured royal patronage of Menander, Buddhist monks settled down to the task of erecting stupas and monasteries. They were in a hurry to capitalise on their great good fortune and unhampered as they were by orthodox Hindu insularity, they had little qualms in using the talents of immigrant craftsmen, better acquainted with Roman and Greek, rather than purely Indian traditions.

The edifice generally known as "The shrine of the Double headed Eagle" at Sirkap (near Taxila) is a square platform faced with local Kanjur stone, adorned with a grid of pilasters of the Roman composite style (Fig. 57). Over this, once stood an elongated version of the Sanchi type stupa that has since vanished. The spaces between the pilasters are filled with reliefs of Roman Classical pedimented aedicule's as well as the indigenous torana, and a chaitya arch. This expedient

56. The 200 B C fire temple of Jandial is a curious mixture of a Greek architectural shell amended for the performances of Zoarastrian rituals 1. Naos. 2. Pronaos 3. Peristyle.

57. Buddha resting within a typical Roman Greco column, capital. The fusion of Indian Roman and Greek traditions is the hall mark of the Gandhara style.

mixing of Romano-Greek and Indian motifs is the embryo of the architectural style that is popularly termed "Gandhara," after the region in which it was born.

The support of Indo-Greek kings to Buddhism was unfortunately short-lived. They had ruled barely for a hundred odd years when a series of chain reactions beyond the frontiers of the country of their adoption brought the armies of the Scythian tribes to the borders of India in 80 B.C.

## THE SCYTHIANS AND KUSHANAS

The Chinese emperor Chi Hsuang Ti, who was responsible for completing the construction of the Great Wall of China, effectively closed off the pastures of China to nomadic tribes of the Yeu-Chi. The Yeu-Chi were forced to press on to the region west of the Aral Sea, original homeland of the Scythians. The displaced Scythians in turn overran Parthia (the northern regions of modern Persia) and Bactria and swept into India probably through the Bolan Pass near Quetta. They had little difficulty in defeating Hippostratus, the last known Greek King.

The brief rule of the Scythians, or Shakas as they came to be known, did not leave any impression on the Buddhist architecture of the times. The classically inspired Fire Temple of about this period, at Jandial near Taxila (Fig. 56) is a curious mixture of a Greek motivated architectural shell for the performance of Achmenid Persian religious rituals. In plan, it is a classic Greek peripteral temple in antis, with columns of the Ionic order. There is, however, no imagery and the platform at the back of the temple suggests the presence of a wooden fire tower dedicated to Mazda, a god of the Zoarastrian pantheon, probably worshipped by the Scythians and Parthians.

The rule of the Shakas in this region was put to an end by their old tormentors, the Yeu-Chi. Led by Kujala Kadphises, they descended through the legendary Khyber Pass about 50 A.D. The Shakas retreated to seek their fortune deeper into western India where they were ultimately absorbed into the Hindu fold. The invaders in the north-west established themselves as the well-known Kushan dynasty of Indian history.

The greatest of the Kushan kings was Kanishka, who ascended the throne in 78 A.D. and ruled over a kingdom, that extended in the south up to Sanchi, in the east to modern Varanasi and in the north-west included the entire Gandhara region. The two great focci of this empire were the cities of Purushapura (modern Peshawar) and the famous Mathura on the banks of the Yamuna. The favours of an emperor as powerful as Kanishka were eagerly sought by both the Brahmins and the Buddhists. Mahayana Buddhism with its direct, more simple approach had a stronger appeal for this great warrior King than the involved metaphysical theories of the Brahmins, overlaid as they were by innumerable and vexatious caste restrictions.

Asvaghosa, himself, a Brahmin convert, was ultimately able to persuade the emperor to adopt Buddhism as his state creed. In Kanishka, Mahayana Buddhism had won a patron of as great significance as Asoka was to Buddhism in its early days. It was at the behest of Kanishka that the fourth and last Great Council of the Buddhists was held at Kundalavana monastery in Kashmir, a perennial favourite of these central Asian kings. Much like the later Moghuls, the Kushan kings often retired to the sylvan valley, to escape the dreaded heat and dust of the Indian plains.

## PROSPERITY UNDER KANISHKA

Kanishka's empire was, if anything, richer than Asoka's. In the wake of the unending foreign invasions of the Greeks, Parthians, Scythians and the Kushanas, trade routes, both by land and sea, had opened up to the west. The Kushanas were on excellent terms with the Romans, the borders of the empires at one time being just 600 miles apart. An immense volume of condiments, spices, unguents and silk left from the ports of later day Gujarat and Sindh coasts, in exchange for Roman sureis, Greek wines and "choice girls for the royal harems."

Such lucrative overseas trade gave rise to a prosperous commercial class. The Buddhists were fortunate in enjoying dual patronage; that of the state, and of their ever dependable allies, the mercantile community. They were busy building once again. Over a period of a couple of hundred years, a number of richly patterned stucco painted and even gilded shrines and monasteries of the Buddhists dotted the otherwise "bare crests and featureless slopes of the Gandhara countryside."

## MONASTERY OF TAKHT-E-BAHI

One of the more impressive and schematically planned of these settlements was built at Takht-e-Bahi (modern Peshwar) (Fig. 58). A 50 feet (15.2 metres) high elongated boat keel profiled stupa, rested on a 20 feet (6 metres) wide square platform, set within a 45 feet (13.7 metres) by 55 feet (16.7 metres) quadrangle along the periphery of which were subsidiary chapels, housing the Bodhisattavas of the Mahayana creed. The roofs of the cells of the surrounding chapels were

58. The Takhte-Bahi monastery near modern Peshawar, nestling between bare hillsides, typical of the Gandhara countryside.

alternately, a dome derived from the shape of the rural beehive hut, and a barrel-vault derived from the roof of the chaitya. Constructed in stone, the roof shapes were built up by means of corbelling, rather than true arching. The masonry, with various sizes of stone arranged in a diaper fashion, was covered with a thick layer of lime plaster relieved with stucco decorations.

59. 1. Court of the stupa, 2. Monasteries, 3. Assembly hall, 4. Refractory and 5. Vestment chambers of Takhte-Bahi monastery.

60. The Buddhist builder was encouraged to elongate his stupa into a vertical monument so that it would be distinguishable from the gently rolling Gandhara countryside.

The central axis of the court of the stupa leads to the familair monastery, which is a series of cells around its own quadrangle (Fig.59). In between the stupa court and the monastery court is an open terrace adorned with small chapels and votive stupas. Around this well knit plan of the central area, are other haphazardly situated ancillary structures, such as an assembly hall, refractory and vestment chambers.

## THE ALI MASJID STUPA

The better preserved, Ali Masjid-Stupa in the Khybar Pass, gives a clearer idea of the decorative scheme of the Gandhara stupas. The stucco frieze applied to the base of the drum is a series of chaitya arches, supported on Corinthian pilasters, each niche being filled with a Grecian version of the different aspects of the deified Buddha of Mahayana.

The stupa, as may be seen, was gradually being transformed from the domical into an elongated and vertical structure (Fig. 60). Apart from the almost primitive desire to make a religious memorial ascend towards the skies, this transformation may well have been influenced by the environment.

The traditional white hemispherical mound, that was a sufficiently striking element in the plains, would have merged inconspicuously, into the slopes of the bare hillsides. However, the bell shaped stupa stood out against the background of a rolling countryside. The vertical umbrella and harmika at the top, gradually came to dominate the entire composition, often becoming taller than the brick and plaster mound, over which it was mounted. As can be seen, this was not an altogether pleasing or logical architectural composition (Fig. 61). Obviously, the aim of the builders was to create taller and taller buildings, without too much attention to the aesthetics of proportion.

61. Platforms in the Greek tradition became the base over which stupas with an elongated umbrella were planted. This accent on height culminated in the design of the famous Chinese pagodas.

## THE PROTOTYPE OF THE PAGODA

The passion for verticality, culminated in a tower, said to have been built by Kanishka in the first century near modern Peshawar. All traces of it, except the ruins of its base have vanished. It was a veritable Buddhist wonder of the world.

As Shun Yat Sen, a Chinese pilgrim of the 6th century testifies, the timber tower of this structure was 628 feet (190.7 metres) high consisting of 13 receding storeys. The whole was surmounted by an iron pinnacle which was adorned with copper gilt umbrellas. It rested on a massive 285×285 feet (86×86 metres) platform of brick and was ultimately destroyed by an attack of lightning, sometime in the 7th century. Chinese pilgrims, facilitated by the contacts of the Kushana with Chinese emperors, had before its collapse carried descriptions of the marvellous edifice to their homeland, where the design took root and under the genius of the Chinese carpenters, flowered into the familiar pagodas of China.

## MAHAYANA SCHOOL OF MATHURA

Mathura, the more centrally situated city of the Kushan Empire was also humming with Buddhist, and even Jain, architectural activity. The building style here was more indigenous, inspired as it was by the art of Sanchi and Bharhut. The spiritual content, however, was of the Mahayana School. Fa Hien, another contemporary Chinese pilgrim to the holy land of Buddhism, saw over a score of monasteries in Mathura inhabited by more than 300 monks. A number of stupas and towers were also erected. These, unfortunately, were so thoroughly demolished by the iconoclastic zeal of later invaders, that not a single complete building of this period has survived.

## END OF THE KUSHAN DYNASTY

Kanishka's long and prosperous reign came to an end in 162 A.D. when he died at war with the Chinese somewhere in central Asia. He was succeeded by his sons Vanishka and Havishka who remained patrons of Buddhism. But the Kushan empire was being threatened from the west by the newly rising and powerful Persian dynasty of the Sassanians. The last Kushan King, who had even taken on the Indian name of Vasudeva was pushed east of the Indus, and ruled for a short period over a small kingdom around Mathura.

With the end of the Kushana dynasty in 220 A.D., the trans-Indus region had once again passed under Persian dominance and was cut off, for some time to come, from the mainstream of Indian history.

# 8

# The "Sanskrit" Brahminism of the Guptas

## Sombre "Garbha-Grihas" and joyous Ajanta

LOOKING back southwards, we find that the power of the once great Andhras was also wilting under the pressure of various burgeoning dynasties of the Deccan. When the major powers of the north-west and south-central India collapsed simultaneously in about 220 A.D., the two empires were dismembered into a number of provincial kingdoms whose rulers had been chafing under the centralised power of the Kushans and Andhras. The Kushan empire gave way to the Yaudehas and Malavas in Rajasthan and to the Nagas, Uccakalpas and Lichhavis in central and eastern India. Suzerainty over the former Andhra country was now shared by the Vakatakas, Chalukayans and Sakas, while the southern tip of the country passed into the control of the Pandyas. The central-southern area fell to the Gangas and Kadambas, the Pallavas holding the south-eastern coast.

### PROSPEROUS ALL-ABSORBING HINDUISM

A number of dynasties, like those of the Sakas, Yaudehas, Vakatakas, and some believe even the Pallavas, were all descendants of various tribes that had been successively pouring into India through its north-west defences only over the last couple of hundred of years. Like the Sakas, they had been gradually pushed deeper into India by subsequent invaders and ultimately carved out a niche for themselves in the complex all-absorbing structure of Hindu society. The country of their adoption was at this time riding the crest of an economic resurgence. It had accumulated tremendous wealth through its trade with the contemporary Romans, Arabs and even the south-east nations of Java, Bali and Sumatra. The rulers of these essentially immigrant dynasties were therefore keen to identify themselves completely with India and to share fully in the material wealth and prosperity of the country.

The feudal kings, following the lead of Kanishka, were beginning to adopt Sanskrit, spoken by the Aryan Brahmin, as their official court language. Since Buddhism had already acquired the status of a world, rather than an Indian religion, Brahmins were quick to present themselves as the only bonafide torch-bearers of a truly indigenous culture to appeal to the prurient interests of the settled tribes and the chauvinism of the ancient Indians. Moreover, in this time of prosperity and optimism, the Brahmins' attitude of "God is Great, Glorious, Gracious! God's work are wonderful. God is love! He is so overwhelmingly adorable that His beings can but sing hymns in His glorification," was a more appealing

61a. Facade of Buddhist cell at Ajanta.

religious attitude to adopt than the comparatively pessimistic outlook and austere message of Buddhism.

Until recently, the Tamil-speaking kingdoms of the south had been at constant and ferocious war with each other, even indulging in acts of cannibalism. They were, however, now organising and uniting themselves into a maritime power to acquire wealth through overseas trade. With growing prosperity the southerners too, were attracted by the cultured and courtly ways of the north and began to adopt what may be called Indo-Aryan attitudes. The seeds of a nation-wide revival of Brahminism, popularly referred to as "Hinduism", were beginning to take root.

## CHANDRAGUPTA

Initially, the Vakatakas tried to take advantage of this undercurrent of national unity, and weld the small kingdoms together into a Hindu empire. The task was, however, ultimately accomplished by Chandragupta, a feudal Raja of ancient Magadha. He emerged out of obscurity, by capitalising on his marriage to a princess of the distinguished and ancient clan of the Lichhavis in 320 A.D. In his short reign of just a decade he became lord of Bihar and parts of Bengal and the Ganges plain, founding the dynasty of the Imperial Guptas. This dynasty, heralded what has popularly come to be known as the "Golden age of India." Chandragupta's son Samudragupta, continued to capitalise on his Lichhavi blood, and in the course of the next 50 years led his armies to distant parts of India. He conquered most of northern India and made the rulers of Assam, Nepal, Kanauj and Punjab his tributaries. The Sakas of western India who had survived the invasions of Samudragupta were finally subdued by his son Chandragupta II the Great, who raided even as far afield as Afghanistan. He even brought the powerful Vakatakas and Kadambas into his fold through matrimonial alliances.

By the beginning of the 5th century A.D. the empire of the Guptas was beginning to show shades of the Mauryas, shades only, for the Guptas in spite of their far flung conquests, found it difficult to install centralised authority over proliferating feudalism, like Asoka had been able. Their cultural conquest of India, however, was more effective, based as it was, on the secular and liberal traditions of an aristocratic upper class—a class that was fond of refined manners, poetry, art and conversation in high-flown Sanskrit only.

62. Ter the only example of an extant brick Buddhist Chaitya hall that is now a Hindu temple, the original duly plastered and painted many times over.

## THE BUDDHIST PRESSURE

Direct state patronage of Buddhism may not have been part of the liberal tradition of the times. Nevertheless, the Buddhists were never the victims of a witch hunt by the ruling class, except when the orders of the monks invited imperial retribution by indulging in the craft of politics. The Sanghas or the orders of Buddhist monks, had in fact acquired large tracts of land. These were a permanent source of income for the building of their great monasteries, and now, even educational establishments. The nuclei of what was to expand into the great University of Nalanda and the monastic complexes of Sarnath and Gaya, were in fact established during this period.

## BRICK AND TIMBER CHAITYAS

In terms of wayside shrines however, the Buddhists were still content with building modest chaitya halls. Most of these have vanished but the surviving one as at Ter and Chezarla in the Deccan (Fig.63), are fair examples, though converted now to Brahmin worship. These chaityas were of modest size, the better preserved one, Ter, being only 22 × 35 feet (6.7 × 10.6 metres), in plan (Fig. 62) and 22 feet (6.7 metres) high at its apex. The vaulted roof of the chaityas was constructed by oversailing horizontal courses of brick masonry. A thick layer of plaster inside and out was used to create the curvilinear profile of a vault.

63. The Ter Chaitya hall with later modifications to convert it into a place of Hindu worship (500 A D).

63a. Plan of the group of caves at Ajanta with inset photo of the horseshoe cliffside into which the caves are carved.

## PULSATING FRESCOES OF AJANTA

The Mahayana Buddhists, however, lavished their wealth and new artistic activity on the proven media of rock-cut cave architecture. In 450 A.D. they returned again to the cliffs of Ajanta, abandoned some 200 years earlier by the Hinayana Buddhists, and set about the task of making numerous additions to an already sacred site. The architectural concept of the chaitya halls of the Mahayana followers differs little from the earlier efforts except that images of Buddha became part of the iconographic scheme. The Viharas, however, emerged now as a combination of a place of residence as well as worship (Fig. 64 a, b). Vast square halls were surrounded by colonnades and monks cells. They were entered through verandahs carved out in the face of the cliff and ended at the back, in mini-chapels full of huge images of Buddha and the Bodhisattavas (Fig. 63a, 61a).

64a, & b. A group of cells around a central hall of worship; a typical vihara at Ajanta. Plan above and isometric below.

65. In painting the fresoces at Ajanta, the Buddhist artist with his sharp eye for detail, provided living images of social life in ancient India.

Apart from carving the traditional sun windows over the main entrances and fascimiles of bamboo gable arches over the doors to the cells, the artist of the Gupta period now proceeded to adorn the walls of the viharas with the world famous "frescoes of Ajanta". To achieve the effect his first step was to cover the rough surface of the exposed stone with a layer of clay and cow-dung mixed with chopped straw and rice husk or animal hair, finished with a fine coat of gypsum. The flat surface thus created was ready to paint on. The basic design was outlined in red ochre, and coated with transparent monochrome. Then with colours made from natural dyes he depicted elaborate scenes of kings and queens, soilders and courtesans, monks and merchants, travellers on horse back or in palanquins, in palaces and houses, gardens and forests, set in the flora and fauna of western India (Fig. 65). These frescoes like early Buddhist sculpture are yet another example of how the Indian artist with his sharp eye for detail filled the gap, created by the traditional disdain for history writing, in our knowledge of an ancient Indian society.

The ceiling of the central vihara hall, on the other hand was ornamented by figurative and geometric designs, consciously unrelated to the surrounding architectural elements to create an effect such as would permeate the blossoming gardens in the open to the sky quandrangle of traditional structural monasteries.

To facilitate the artist in executing his ambitions works of art, the darkness of the caves was lit up by reflecting the rays of the sun from large metal mirrors installed outside. Under circumstances more trying than those faced by Michalengelo a thousand years later, the artists of Ajanta produced a complete and colourful array of the every-day life of the leisurely and the wealthy. The caves of the Buddhists had come a long way from the sombre and dignified awe-inspiring halls of Karli to the vibrant and pulsating Viharas of Ajanta.

At the time that Buddhist architecture was reaching the acme of its art, Hindu revival, thriving under the stable rule of Chandragupta II, was seeking an architectural representation for its religious beliefs.

## EARLY HINDU SHRINES

The ritual of the Aryan Hindu had till now involved the propitiation of abstract forms of natural forces. These forces being assumed to be omnipresent, the building of permanent earthly abodes for them had not been found necessary. The only edifice required was an altar, roofed if it at all, with timber posts and beams covered with matted reeds. However, like Mahayana, which in bowing to popular appeal had given in to the worship of images of Buddha, an anthropomorphic conception of a deity in the form of a statue, gradually become a part of Hindu worship too.

The earliest Brahminical or Hindu shrine was nothing more than a cell to house an image. Other rituals were still conducted in the open air. The oldest shrines of the Hindu religion, true to the national genius, are once again a group of caves, carved out of a mountain side at Udaygiri, near ancient Sanchi (Fig. 67). The interior is a plain rectangular room or garbha-griha (literally the womb-house), in which the image was installed. The entrance is through a small portico, which was a faithful representation in stone, of the familiar post and lintel timber model oft-depicted in the paintings of Ajanta.

66. The Gupta temple at Sanchi, inspired as it was by Udayagiri, is a windowless cubic volume with an attached portico.

67. A cave and attached portico at Udayagiri. True to Indian tradition, the earliest place of Hindu worship was a dark cubic space carved out of living rock.

## TEMPLES AT TIGAWA AND SANCHI

The earliest extant structural Hindu temples are at Sanchi and at Tigawa near Jabbalpur. Though their patrons decided to build temples by the more conventional structive methods of masonry, the only model of Hindu sanctums known to the designers were the grottos of Udaygiri. The wheel now seems to have come full circle. We find the structural masonry builder taking his cue from the art of the rock cutter, who centuries ago had modelled his own craft on free standing timber edifices of the Aryan wood worker.

    The Sanchi temple (Fig. 66) of the early fifth century repeats in toto the plan of the Udaygiri shrines. The cell, housing the image, is a dark hollow cube. The meticulously jointed stone block walls of the cell support a roof of flat stone slabs. Derived as it was from the concept of a cave, the craftsmen had not yet developed an aesthetic system to embellish the plain masonry of the outer surface. The pillars of the entrance portico attached to the only opening in the garbhagriha are stunted versions of the familiar free standing Asoka columns, complete with the inverted bell capital and imagery of animal motifs, the only kind of vertical shaft known to the Indian builder.

UDAYGIRI CAVE 1   SANCHI

68. The portico of the Tigawa temple with the typical Gupta column along with a comparative study of contemporary columns.

TIGWA     ERAN

Using stone as a building material for their religious edifices for the first time, the craftsmen unsure of its structural potential were unwilling to take any risks. Even the roof of the small 12 feet (3.6 metres) wide portico is supported on as many as four columns. To allow for a reasonable entrance in the middle though, the columns are erected in pairs, situated at either end of the longer length.

In comparison to this rather subdued effort at Sanchi, the temple at Tigawa, though built on a similar plan, has a refreshing new flourish about it. This is apparent in the novel design of the portico columns (Fig. 68). These are no longer the conventional octogonal shaft of Asoka's period. Rather square in plan they are boldly ornamented with robust sculpture of gods and goddesses of the ever growing Hindu pantheon in flamboyant postures. The design of the capital too, heralds the new Gupta imagery of the Purana kalasa marking the end of the period of the stereotyped inverted bell used consistently for almost 600 years, since Asoka's times. The spirit of the liberal Gupta empire was beginning to percolate down to its craftsmen too. As if drunk with this spirit, they proceeded, as we shall see, to lay the foundations of the burgeoning architectonic symbols of the new and resurgent religion of the Brahmins.

# 9

# The Chalukyas and the Guptas

## Brahmin shrines—North and South

THE empire that Chandragupta and Samudragupta had won through diplomacy and war over a period of 100 years was finally bequeathed to Kumargupta I. During the 40 years of his peaceful rule, the Guptas reached the zenith of their power and splendour. Chandragupta II had earlier at Ujjain, rallied around him the famous "Nine Gems", the greatest intellectual lights of his time, setting the characteristic Gupta life style—"a consciously refined syncretism of method, learned training and self-control." Under Kumargupta, this style acquired an authority over other associate courts, not unlike that wielded by Versailles, in the 17th and 18th centuries, over other European courts.

## HINDU ART PERVADES THE SOUTH

Some sense of this artistic authority, as we shall see, seems to have been felt even in the south. A group of craftsmen were commissioned by their Chalukyan overlords in about 600 A.D. to build shrines, for the Aryan gods, whom they had recently started worshiping, at their capital city of Aihole (in modern Karnataka state). Probably immigrants from the site of Ajanta just over 300 miles north, the craftsmen were familiar with the paraphernalia of Buddhist ritual and well versed in the high traditions of Gupta sculpture. However, they had neither a visual idea nor any experience in the building of free standing monuments, leave aside a specific concept of a Hindu temple. Their client, the Hindu priest, too was as much at sea. He had only the vaguest ideas of what his temple should be—"an impressive structure where a graven image of God could be installed, consecrated and worshipped."

True to instinct, the pioneer builders, picked on the most prestigious rural timber structure, the *"Santhagar,"* or Assembly Hall of the village council, as their model (Fig. 70).

69. The 450 A D temple of Ladkhan as it stands today with its mandapa openings fiilled in with jalis.

70. The "Santhagara" or assembly hall of the village council.

# THE LAD KHAN AT AIHOLE

With a few modifications they set about the task of adapting its timber structural form to the permanency of stone masonry and its village council plan to one fit for the worship of gods. The result of their innocent endeavour is a temple, which for some curious reasons is popularly called the Lad Khan (Fig. 69). In plan (Fig. 71) it is a square hall of 50 feet (15.2 metres) side, roofed with gargantuan sloping stone slabs, simulating the thatch roof of the original. Instead of timber posts to hold up the roof, there is an inner double row of massive stone columns. The peripheral columns are reduced to mere pilasters, the load of the roof being taken up by a wall of cyclopean stone blocks piled one over the other, without binding material. Some of the open panels were filled in years later with stone grills of incongruous designs.

**71**. Ladkhana temple. Showing 1. Garbhagriha, 2. Mandapa and 3. Entrance portico.

72. The Ladkhana temple in bulky ponderous stone, its forms inspired by the thatch and bamboo Santhagara.

In the middle of the rear wall of the main hall a square portion was partitioned off to create a workable equivalent of an inner sanctum, the garbhagriha. The peripheral timber bench with an inclined back (*asana*) that was a functional requirement of the "Santhagar"—was dispensed with in the main hall. In the attached portico however where the worshippers could sit and chat after their ritual was over, even the bench has been reproduced in stone, thereby serving the dual function of a resting place and a baluster. This element of folk architecture in fact was destined to become a major design element in the hands of the classic Hindu architect particularly in the central and western regions of the country.

The Chalukyan builders copied the timber prototype of their choice as faithfully as their Buddhist predecessors. The projecting edges of the slabs of the roof are rounded off to imitate the original thatch over-hang, and even the bamboo ribs holding the thatch down, are reproduced in bulky semi-cylinders of stone (Fig. 72). The result is a building of stark, strong and enduring appearance, relieved but a little by the iconography that displays the unmistakable plastic and sensual grace of the Gupta sculpture at Ajanta. To the Hindu mind already well versed in abstractions, this much too pedantic verisimilitude interpretation of a timber form, was far from the perfect shrine.

# THE DURGA TEMPLE, AIHOLE

Judging from the nearby Durga temple (Fig. 73), the Chalukyan builders in their search for an appropriate monumental shrine tried to adapt the plan of the Buddhist chaitya hall to Hindu worship. In building this temple of Durga, they merely divided the inner colonnaded nave of the chaitya hall into an ante-chamber and sanctuary by putting a platform across near the apsidel end (Fig. 74). The aisles around became an open pradakshina path of sorts. The roof of cumbersome sloping stone slabs displays little advancement over the constructive techniques of the Lad Khan, though this temple was built

73. The 500 A D Durga temple at Aihole, planned like a Buddhist Chaitya hall surrounded by a verandah with gargantaun pillars.

74. The apsidal ended Buddhist Chaitya hall adopted for Hindu worship by creating a garbhagriha where the stupa would have been.

years later. This production of the struggling Chalukyan builder was too obviously derived in all its aspects from the Buddhist chaitya hall. No wonder then that it failed to win Hindu approval as an appropriate sacrosanct edifice. It is apparent that the builders, inexperienced in using stone as a structural material, were unable to create the monuments that the Hindus desired to erect over their cavern of worship. They interpreted the Hindu concept of a temple as a "House of God" rather too literally as just a house and no more. What was apparently missing in these early shrines was an architectonic form that would at once adequately symbolise a new faith and convert the "house" into a virtual monument.

## SOPHISTICATED URBANITY UNDER THE GUPTAS

One such symbol was destined to be developed miles away in the north, where under the Guptas a luxurious style of city life was emerging with most of the paraphernalia of towns and cities familiar to us today. The prosperous urban dweller had acquired the necessary wherewithal to live the life of a dilettante. He was a lover of poetry, painting and music, paid great attention to his sartorial elegance, collected objets d' art of ceramic, copper and iron and patronised courtesans versed in the refined arts as well as the techniques of love expounded in the now famous Hindu treatise on sex, the Kamasutra. Towns and cities were developing rapidly to cater to the needs of such a society. Though society was not yet divided into the rigid Hindu caste system of later times, a horizontal stratification by economic status or occupation was beginning to tell.

The affluent section of the city was planned as a series of square or rectangular blocks allocated to the different classes or castes, with houses of varying heights "having balconies or belvederes made of wood" built around open courtyards. The shopping streets had houses for the owners on upper floors; a pattern still followed in the modern Indian bazaars of today. On the outskirts of the planned city "Butchers, dancers, executioners, scavengers and so on have their abodes," made of wattled bamboo much like the shanty towns of today. The larger part of the city was built in timber and brick. The former was abundantly available from the forests around and the sandy clay of the plains was ideal for the baking of the latter using timber as fuel. These were also the most suitable materials for rapid and fairly durable construction.

# BRICK TEMPLE OF BHITARGAON

Over a period of time, bricklayers acquired a great degree of proficiency in their craft and were eventually called in by the Brahmin aristocracy to build temples for them. An early extant example of the bricklayers skills, is a temple (Fig. 77) at Bhitargaon, (in the modern Rampur district). It is built upon a substantial plinth and rises some 40 feet high. Structurally it is an interesting building, in its use of soundly constructed brick domes and vaults for its main cell and vestibule. The detailing of the surfaces with richly moulded surfaces (Fig.76) gradually ascending to a barrel vaulted top, is executed by craftsmen whose technical versatility is undeniable.

The silhouette of the Bhitargaon temple (Fig. 75) however leaves the impression of a rather ponderous and ungainly pile of masonry. What is more, the shape of the mound over the main cell is clearly inspired by the barrel vault roof of the Buddhist chaitya hall, a building form which even the Buddhists had dropped from their priorities, almost a century earlier. However ungraceful the building, it did manage to convey the essential idea of monumentality, by its sheer bulk and height. Over the years, the Hindu craftsman was slowly creeping towards a solution to his problem.

75. Bhitargaon temple of 550 A D an example of the brick masons attempts at creating an appropirate towering mass for the Hindu temple.

76. The brick layers treated the facade much like stone carvers by cutting and embossing sculptural patterns into the masonry.

77. In plan this brick temple at Bhitargaon consists only of a—1. Garbhagriha and 2. Entrance portico.

78. The famous shikhara, in its earliest glory. From all evidence it would seem that the earliest most perfect and symmetrically organised example of the shikhara, that was destined to crown the myriads of Hindu temples all over the country, was evolved in 500 AD at Deogarh in central India.

## EVOLUTION OF THE SHIKHARA

It surely was some anonymous genius who, with a deep insight into the Aryan Hindu mind and an equally profound appreciation of its architectural potential, came up with the form of the parabolic profiled Shikhara. The many variations of this pinnacle devised over the ensuing years, adorn all Hindu places of worship in the north, that have any pretentions to being a temple, to date. Whether the inspiration for the form of the Shikhara came from the profile of the traditional mythological abode of the gods, the snow clad peaks of Himalayas or from the primitive megaliths or toda churches of central India (Fig. 79) or from the shape of the traditional Indian wooden *ratha* (Fig. 80) or chariot or from a rural Aryan form, since "all Indian art derives from the Aryan village," there is little doubt that the designer came up with a form that is a puzzling and intriguing mixture of geometry and mythological symbolism. Over the evolution of such a form, many an architectural theoretician has broken his head. However, the simplest way to describe this form is as a four sided pyramid with parabolic instead of straight edges (Fig. 81). Its curvilinear shape also strongly suggests its derivation from a bamboo construction most likely that of four bamboos rising from a square base, held together at an appropriate height directly above the middle of the square (Fig. 82). It was decided to mount this parabolic form over the roof of the cube of the garbha-griha or the inner sanctum.

It is quite likely that initial experiments with this kind of shrine may well have been made with timber shikharas over dolmen shrines in stone. However, the earliest surviving classical form of it is of course a temple constructed in stone at Deogarh (Fig. 78) in central India. A step by step evolution of its design is easy to follow.

**79, 80, 81 & 82.** The ratha, the toda church and bamboo roof that may have inspired the builders to create the form of the shikhara.

The early Sanchi or Tigawa type dolmen shrine was the starting point. Complete with its attached portico, this was placed on a wide square platform inspired no doubt by the sacred sacrificial altars of the vedic Aryans. For reasons of symmetry, a false portico was attached to each of three otherwise blank walls of the cubic garbha-griha. What appear to be door ways are in fact porticos housing beautifully sculptured stone panels instead of timber shutters (Fig. 83). The flat roof of the

83. One of the three sculptured panels that adorn the false porticos of the Deogarh temple.

dolmen was now surmounted by an architecturalised form of convex profiled pyramid. This was built in discernible horizontal course of receding stone slabs approximating to the cambered outline of the bamboo prototype. At the apex of this spire was mounted a large circular disc of stone into the rim of which was inscribed vertical edges like in an "amlaka" fruit; a fruit that plays a symbolic role in various Hindu rituals. This total composition, including the inevitable metal pinnacle or "kalasa" over the amlaka, is what came to be classified as the legendary Shikhara (literally mountain peak).

The designers had at last after years of endeavour evolved an acceptable new and distinguished architectonic symbol for the Hindu temple. The shikhara by its more frequent usage in the north was destined to become the distinctive feature of the North-Indian temple. Classical writers in identifying the north with Aryan traditions conveniently refer to it as the most prominent feature of the Indo-Aryan temple style; a style that, as we shall see, was destined to give rise to the many famous regional styles of Rajasthan, Gujarat, Khajuraho and Orissa.

# 10

## Harsha - the last great Buddhist

### Sarnath, Gaya and Nalanda

FA-HIEN, a Chinese Buddhist pilgrim of the Gupta period traversed the entire length of India from west to east at the beginning of 5th century A.D. He records with evident gratification that throughout his journey, extending over a decade he was never once molested or attacked. Under the rule of the Guptas which lasted almost to the end of the 5th century "India was perhaps the happiest and most civilised region of the world for the effete Roman empire was nearing its destruction and China was passing through a time of troubles."

## MIHIRGULA THE HUN

Troubles across the borders, however, meant trouble for India as well. The central Asian nomads, this time the tribe of the Hunas, were on the move again. The Gupta Empire withstood their pressure long enough to divert the greatest of their fury towards Europe. Ultimately in about 500 A.D. after defeating the Sassanians of Iran, Tormana the Huna established his capital in ancient Sagala the former capital of King Menander. His son, Mihirgula, a monster of iniquity to the Buddhists, turned upon them with great savagery, destroying many of their monastic establishments in the Gandhara region and slaughtering the inmates. Monasteries like the Takhte-Bahi, which survived this holocaust, though in a ruinous state, have already been described.

Mihirgula's reign of terror, though ferocious, was fortunately short-lived. A confederacy of Hindu Kings led by Yashodharaman of Kanauj, finally forced him to seek shelter in the valley of Kashmir, where he died before he was able to renew his attacks in the plains below. And, once again now, for over a hundred years India succumbed to the turmoils of a long period of unproductive feudalism. Finally, Prince Harsha of Thanesar (north of modern Delhi), through a series of fortutious circumstances ascended the throne of Kanauj in A.D. 630. Over the next six years Harsha "went from east to west subduing all who were not obedient." After this incessant campaign, much like Asoka, he "reigned in peace for thirty years without striking a blow."

There is probably some truth in the story that Harsha when a lad of sixteen had entertained ideas of entering a Buddhist monastery. Circumstances catapulted him into accepting the responsibilities of a Hindu Kshatriya King, but his faith in the "Middle Path" shown by Buddha, was obviously unshaken. It was under his reign that Buddhism had its last days

**84.** The brick remains of the splendid stupa that was the monument magnificient of the once great Nalanda establishment, of about 500 A D.

of glory in India. By this time, the religion had gained a large following not only in the north-western region of modern Afghanistan, but also eastwards in Burma, South Asia and northwards across the Himalayas in China. India and particularly the region of the modern Bihar (from the so many Buddhist "Viharas" that dotted the countryside of the region) was to the Buddhist world at large, like Jerusalem to the Christians. Pilgrims and scholars were beginning to pour in to India in search of solace or knowledge. The phenomena saw the blossoming of places associated with historic incidents in Buddha's life into centres of holy pilgrimage. Most popular of these are places like Kapilavastu, the place of the "Nativity", Budh Gaya, the scene of enlightenment and Sarnath where the first sermon was delivered. Centres of learning such as that at Nalanda established years ago were now assuming worldwide importance, with students from far away lands seeking theological training in the land of the birth of the Buddha.

85. The accretion of stupas, temples and monastries at Sarnath, where Buddha hundreds of years earlier, had given his first sermon.

## BUDH GAYA AND SARNATH

The two great centres of pilgrimage were Budh Gaya and Sarnath. Sarnath (near modern Varanasi) at one time was a thriving and bustling monastic complex. A number of stupas, stambhas, toranas and many storeyed viharas accumulated on this holy site over hundreds of years, much like at Sanchi unguided it would seem by an overall master plan of any sort (Fig. 85). The Mahayana School having acquired prominence, the emphasis was shifting from Chaityas to temples built after the fashion of Hindu shrines, since instead of worshipping the Stupa, the image of Buddha itself was venerated, not unlike the craven image of a Hindu god.

The tower of the temple at Sarnath, with its seven clearly marked receding storeys, rising to a height of 110 feet (33.4 metres) derives inspiration both from the elongated stupas of Gandhara as well as the shikharas of Hindu shrines. At the apex of the pyramid was mounted a miniature stupa, and harmika pinnacle, to distinguish it from a Hindu temple. The nearby Dhamek stupa (Fig. 86), now in a ruinous state, on the other hand is more distinctly derived from the style of Gandhara. The hemispherical mound of brick was raised over

86. The form of the Dhamek stupa of 700 A D now in ruins was probably inspired by the Gandhara style raised as it is over a tall cylindrical base.

a tall cylindrical base. The four cardinal points of the substructure are decorated with pilastered and arched niches which at one time were filled with large image of Buddha.

The shrine of Budh Gaya (Fig. 88) being a single large complex displays a more definite sense of design. The 180 feet (54.7 metres) high temple spire (Fig. 87) is the focus of the rather inconsequential modern structure around it. This temple was restored, under the supervision of General Cunningham of the Archeological Survey of India, in 1881. Much of the original which may have been centuries older, has been covered up. The restoration featured the building of a broad terrace at the base of the temple. At the corners of the platform, towers echoing the shape of the main spire were built up to conform to the panchratna concept of planning. General Cunningham's work has been the subject of heated controversy among historians and archaeologists. In its original form, the temple without the corner towers is conjectured to have been cordoned off only by the traditional Vedika, with may be a torna to mark the entrance. The shape of the original temple tower was probably not substantially different from that of Sarnath, described earlier.

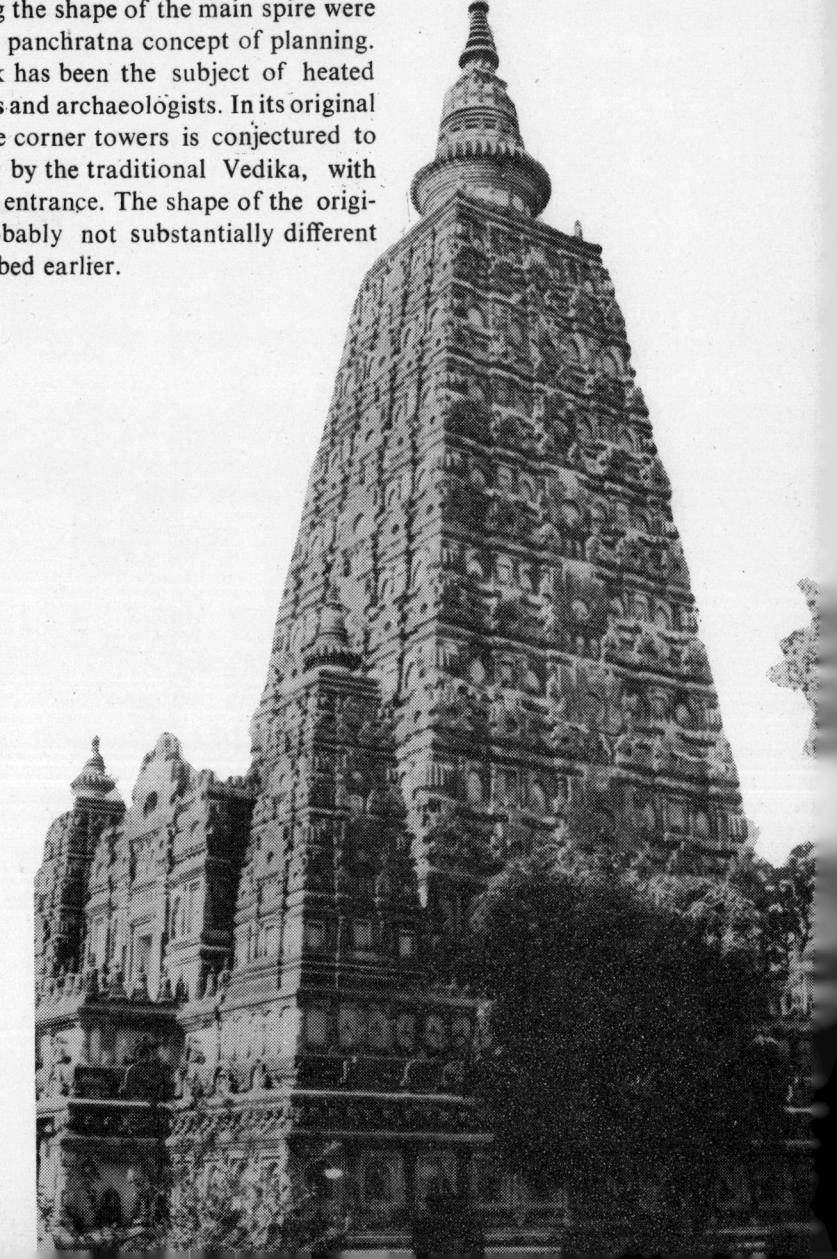

87. The spire of the Bodh Gaya temple, rebuilding of which in 1881, caused great controversy regarding the original design and General Cunningham's restoration.

## THE GREAT UNIVERSITY OF NALANDA

For architectural magnificence however, in its heyday the Buddhist University at Nalanda, near modern Patna, overshadowed both Sarnath and Budh Gaya. The most prominent feature at Nalanda was a massive stupa (Fig. 84) of which only the most incomprehensible ruins of the successive accretions are extant. When complete it was more than 110 feet (33.4 metres) high and rested on a 30 feet (9.1 metres) high, 100 feet (30.4 metres) square platform. It was approached by a broad imposing flight of steps, rising up from a central avenue. The walls of the base of the stupa were divided with cornices into horizontal friezes, further partitioned vertically into pilastered niches, containing either the sun window emblem or images of Buddha. At the corners of the main platform were buttresses

88. The plan of the Bodh Gaya shrine is akin to that of a Hindu temple though it has all the symbolic trappings of a Buddhist shrine.

in the form of turrets crowned by mini-stupas. This Panch-ratna (five jewels) concept of planning consisting of a central shrine and four subsidiary ones at the corners (Fig. 90) became the essence of design of the Buddhist style of architecture that flourished subsequently in south-east Asia. The famous temple at Angkor Vat in Cambodia is the most glorious of these.

## THE PLANNING OF THE CAMPUS

The rows of such magnificent stupas placed side by side formed the central monumental axis of the Nalanda complex (Fig. 89). Parallel to, and on both sides of this axis were what may be called "avenues of the monasteries", since on either side of these were establishments housing students aspiring to become monks. These monasteries or viharas, (a heap of ruins now, built as they were in brick and timber) were planned in the usual manner around a central open court. They functioned both as units of residence as well as learning. The lower storeys contained the refectory, areas of instructions and communal worship while the upper floor built in timber was a quadrangle of cells for resident students. Each subsequent higher storey was stepped back from the previous one to create open air terraces for the cells. Also it is said, the higher storeys with smaller number of cells housed the more persevering students who had graduated to an advanced stage of learning.

89. The orderly layout of "colleges", hostels and dormitories along the classic avenues of learning that were the core of the campus of the Nalanda University which in its heyday was "richly adorned by towers and fairy like turrets."

90. The Angkor Vat in Cambodia, that was the culmination of the Panchratna concept of Buddhist planning.

A number of such monasteries were built close to each other like so many colleges in a university campus. Complemented by the white and gilded domes of the stupa, rising into the sky, they were seen by the famous Chinese pilgrim Hiuan Tsang in the 7th century before they were razed to the ground by the Muslim invaders of the 11th century. "The richly adorned towers, and the fairy-like turrets" he says, "like pointed hill tops are congregated together. The observatories seem to be lost in vapours of the morning, and the upper rooms tower above the clouds. The outside courts in which are the priest chambers are in four stages and have dragon projections and coloured eaves, the pearl red pillars carved and ornamented, the richly adorned balustrades and roofs covered with tiles that reflect the light in a thousand ways, these things add to the beauty of the scene." This, however, as we shall see, was destined to be the last "beautiful scene" of Buddhist architecture in India. While Buddhism took root in the various eastern and south eastern countries to blossom into a creed that is still a living religion, in India the psychological onslaught of the Brahmins ultimately prevailed. The history of Indian architecture for over 500 years hereafter is virtually the story of the blossoming of the Hindu temple into great cathedrals.

# 11

# The Chalukya Pallava Power Balance

## Shrines of Aihole, Badami and Mahabalipuram

AIHOLE remained the capital of the Chalukya kings, till the first Pulakesin's son Mangalisa shifted it to nearby Vitapi (modern Badami) in 578 A.D. Aihole, as we have seen, was the site of the early experiments in Hindu temple building which had resulted in the rather lack-lustre shrines of Lad Khan and Durga. Badami, the new capital, was picturesquely located on a lake, surrounded by steeply rising cliffs, like those of the Western Ghats and Ajanta.

### ROCK-CUTTING AT BADAMI

As was to be expected, rock cutters were soon at work carving out halls from the scarp of hill overlooking the southeast of the town. Like their predecessors at Aihole, their notions of the appropriate form for a Hindu shrine were quite vague. The typical Hindu and Jain cave sanctum of Badami (Fig. 91) therefore turned out to be nothing more than

91. A facade of the rock cut Hindu cave at Badami, and left an overall view of the ancient town of Badami.

an outer pillared-verandah, through which one entered a colonnaded hall to worship the Shiva Linga in a cell of sorts, right at the back The builders had done no more than make "additions and alterations" to the plan of an Ajanta vihara to make it into a workable Hindu shrine. While the rock cutters patiently carved out a row of such, rather insipid, cave temples, the never-say-die stone masons of Aihole, turned their attentions to adding lustre to the architectural qualities of the rather non-descript existing edifices; the well known Lad Khan and Durga at Aihole.

92. The shikhara having been accepted as the appropriate symbol of Hindu faith was planted over existing temples such as the Durga at Aihole.

## ADDITIONS TO DURGA AND LAD KHAN

In the Durga temple, the eminently successful shikhara the form of which had already been developed in the north was rather incongruously planted over the apsidal end of the flat roof (Fig. 92). The Lad Khan on the other hand was adorned with a cubic volume built over the central flat portion of the roof over the main hall (Fig. 93). In both cases, no doubt the height of the original was enhanced. This alone, however, could not be expected to produce an architectural composition of distinctive quality. Nevertheless, the latter effort proved to be not entirely in vain. The design of an old temple, now virtually in ruins, on a ledge of rock overlooking Badami, is quite likely an inspired though radically modified version of the profiles of the Lad Khan.

93. Instead of the shikhara, a cubic volume was planted over the Ladkhan in an attempt to give height and architectural eminence to a rather ordinary shrine.

# THE EVOLUTION OF THE "VIMANA"

The designer of this unnamed temple (Fig. 94) seems to have reorganised the rather disparate elements of the Lad Khan into an integrated whole. The garbhargriha which had been an incongruously partitioned space in the rear of the Lad Khan, is appropriately relocated at the core of the composition. The aisles so formed around the cella became an enclosed pradakshina path, roofed though, like in its prototype, with massive sloping slabs of stone. The ground plan (Fig. 95) is completed by the addition of a small mandap or ante-room preceding the garbhagriha, and an entrance portico similar to that of the Lad Khan.

94, 95, 96, 97. The plan, sectional restored view and other details of the ruined temple at Badami, that forms an essential link in tracing the design development of the South Indian vimana

It is however the design of the dolmen addition over the garbhagriha (Fig. 96) and the conscious shedding of obvious folk art trappings of the Lad Khan temple that mark a decisive step in the evolution of classical temple architecture in the south. The tower now takes the form of a stepped pyramid, every step defined by horizontal mouldings of varying thickness. Each one though is rounded off, as if to consciously remind the viewer of its origins from the gentle overhang of the thatch roofs over bamboo huts. The apex is crowned by a domical form, derived as ever from a rural one. In this case, the architects preferred the shallow almost semicircular contours of a bamboo canopy, built up over a square base (Fig. 97). With minimal modifications this curvilinear form was hewn out of massive blocks of masonry and planted squat over the tower.

The combination of a stepped pyramid and dome with a cubic or prismatic base, even in its primitive form was a novel and pleasing ensemble. It was to become the hallmark of south Indian temple architecture, symbolising the Shaivite aspect of the Hindu trinity, which enjoyed great popularity in the south just as the Vaishnavite enjoyed in the north.

The pyramidal tower (popularly known as the Vimana in south Indian architectural terminology) crowning the temple of Badami though was far from perfect. The inexperienced hands of the stone mason, working with large unwieldy blocks of stone had given birth to a new concept but refinements of detail and the fluidity of the profile of the vimana was to be achieved by another group of craftsmen elsewhere in India.

# THE MIGRANT CRAFTSMEN

Meanwhile Chalukyan control over Vengi, a large consolidated tract of cultivatable flat land, lying between the Krishna and Godavari rivers, was challenged by the Pallavas of the upper southern coast. The powers of the Chalukyan and Pallavas however were evenly balanced. This resulted in frequent tests of strength between these two major powers of the south. The Pandya, Kadamba and Ganga dynasties of the further south were content to play second fiddle. They supported either side to suit their own political expediency, without losing control over their own smaller kingdoms.

At the conclusion of such battles, skilled craftsmen either transferred their allegiance voluntarily or were often forcibly carried away from the kingdom of the vanquished, to build temples for the victorious king. During this period there was, therefore, a parallel and inter-related growth of temple architecture in the cities of the Chalukyas and Pallavas, since the masons and sculptors who were shunted back and forth belonged to the same school of craftsmanship.

# THE PALLAVAS AND MAHABALIPURAM

Mahabalipuram was the coastal capital of the early Pallavas. Situated at the mouth of the Palar river, it stood on a 100 feet (33.3 metre) high, and a half mile (800 metre) long hill of granite gneiss rising out of the surrounding sands. The citadel on top of the mound was secured by impressive fortifications. The administration offices and residences for merchants and members of the ruling class, located around the central place, were built over stone basements, some of which have survived to this date. The superstructures, presumably of timber and brick, have vanished. The remnants of water channels and conduits show that the town was served by an elaborate and well designed system of water supply and drainage.

Mahendra Verman II, one of the Pallava rulers of the early seventh century, and a contemporary of Harshvardhana of Thanesar, was the major figure responsible for the political and cultural growth of the Tamil country. Though born Jaina he was converted to Shaivism quite early in his life. He displayed an unusual interest in the arts, being himself a poet and even the author of a play entitled "The Delights of the Drunkard" (Mattavilass Prahasana). It was under his patronage that a novel and significant experiment in the art of temple building in the south was carried out.

## GUILDS OF MASONS AND CUTTERS

It is quite likely that by now, two disinct guilds of building craftsmen had evolved; that of stone masons and stone carvers, each proud of its own tradition and ever eager to challenge the other. Aware of the aesthetic shortcomings of the efforts of the former at Aihole and Badami, the latter were now commissioned by the Pallavas. In an attempt to prove their virtuosity they created in one spot a multitude of forms and shapes that the "ideal" Hindu temple could take. A small granite outcrop, about 250 feet (75.2 metres) long and 30 feet (9.1 metres) high south of the fortifications of Mahabalipuram became the site of the most unusual experiment in the techniques of building, resulting in a form of architecture that flourished into a mature and consummate art in India, but without parallel outside.

## FREE STANDING MONOLITHS

Instead of carving caves out of the living rock as his forebears had done for centuries in India, the sculptor architect, with surprising aplomb proceeded to chisel down the granite outcrop into free standing monolithic models of structural buildings much like the romantic gardner pares thick hedges into shapes of animals and birds. The stone carvers' perseverance resulted in the famous seven Pagodas or Rathas (literally chariots) of Mahabalipuram (Fig. 98). Due to the

98. The Pallava builders added an altogether new dimension to the art of rock cutting in India, when in 650 A.D. they chose to cut down an outcrop of living rock into rathas of various shapes and designs—the famous seven rathas of Mahabalipuram.

disposition of the outcrop,— a narrow and long whale-backed hump of none too great dimension—the seven virtual architectural models are of moderate size and aligned along a single axis. Though for some obscure historic reasons, the work of finishing and polishing "the models" was abandoned, the artists managed to present to the king an array of distinctly comprehensible temple forms. Each of these eight was subsequently named after the heroes of the great Hindu epic, the Mahabharata.

## THE RATHAS OF MAHABALIPURAM

Draupadi, (Fig. 99), the simplest of the so called Rathas, is an unpretentious version of the rural portable wooden shrine with a square base and curvilinear thatch roof. Three others are varying interpretations of the Buddhist chaitya hall. The most elementary of these is rectangular in plan with a peripheral colonnade covered with a barrel vaulted roof, yet another the Sahadeva (Fig.100) mounts a three tiered roof over an apsidal ended plan, culminating into the barrel vaulted chaitya form at the apex. In the Ganesh Ratha, (Fig. 101), a rectangular entrance portico is attached to the already complex ensemble of forms of the Sahadeva Ratha.

Though the forms of the Bhima, Sahadeva and Ganesh ratha were also absorbed into the myriads of forms of the later temple architecture of the south, the form of the Dharmaraj proved to be the "King" among all (Fig. 102). Built over a square plan, it was found to do the greatest aesthetic justice to all the formal, cosmological and ritual requirements of a temple, as explained in detail in a later chapter on the theories of Hindu architecture. Each receding level (*Bhumi*) of the pyramidal roof of the Dharamraj, is in itself a miniature model of the Buddhist vihara (Fig. 103). What were cells for the residence of the monk in the original, are here frozen into either miniature ornamental domes or barrel vaulted turrets. The place of the central open court of the living vihara, is taken up by a solid core of rectangular masonry

99, 100, 101, 102. The Draupadi, Sahadeva, Ganesh and Bhim rathas at Mahabalipuram.

103. Dharmaraja the supreme ratha that was ultimately adopted as the most appropriate form of the vimana to crown the South Indian Hindu temple.

diminishing in size as it approaches the apex. The finial of this finely proportioned and meticulously carved pyramid is an elegantly contoured ribbed octagonal dome, poised over a squat cylindrical shaft. The whole in fact is a perfectly sculptured crystallisation of the rather cumbersome structural efforts of the builders of Badami.

The Chalukyan builder and the Pallava sculptor had thus between themselves evolved an appropriately aesthetic spire (Vimana) for the garbhagriha of the south Indian temple.

# 12

# The Triumphant Pallavas and Rasthrakutas

## Building at Kanchipuram and carving at Ellora

FLUSHED with the triumph of his artists, Mahendra Verman's successor Rajasimha, proceeded to dot the eastern coast line and his new 7th century capital of Kanchipuram with "structive" temples, that were variations on the Dharmaraja theme.

### SHORE TEMPLE, MAHABALIPURAM

The most exquisite and well preserved of these is the "Shore temple" at Mababalipuram (Fig. 104). Delicately poised on the rocky shoreline, half in the sea and half on land, the main sanctury of the temple looks out towards the sea while a subsidiary one faces the shore. Such an arrangement was necessitated by its peculiar location since the entrance to the former became flooded and unapproachable at high tide. The spires over either of the cellas, are the earliest and probably the most serene and beautiful examples of soundly structured masonry versions, of the sculptural Dharamaraja Ratha. Though the geometric scheme of these is the same as that of the Dharmaraja, their somewhat elongated profile is like a graceful feminine complement to the strong and robust masculinity of their Dharmaraja prototype.

Both the sancturies and subsidiary mandapas of the temple stood within a walled precinct (Fig. 105). The courtyard of the temple could be partially flooded, by a complex system of channels reservoirs and drains that carried the sea water into basins around the cult room. The Pallavas, a sea-faring people, conducted rituals of worship of water in this temple. To the Pallava mariner, the edifice was a virtual lighthouse. He was guided to his haven of safety by observing a lamp lit on a pillar in the courtyard that could be seen from the ocean through an aperture in the wall. The quality of the construction of the shore temple marks the graduation of the south Indian stone mason from an initiate, into an accomplished craftsman.

The shore temple at Mahabalipuram on the Eastern coast of India built half into the sea and half on land.

Plan of the shore temple at Mahabalipuram showing location of two shrines back to back.

PLAN.

THE SHORE TEMPLE MAHABALIPURAM.

Rajasimha now attempted to build an even larger temple, the Kailash Nath, within his new capital city of Kanchipuram. In order to enlarge the base of the temple, the architects appended mini-rathas at the corners and middle of the four walls of the cella; a none too successful experiment that was never repeated. The contours and details of the stepped pyramid of the tower, however, conforms to that of the Dharmaraja vimana, which obviously had won acceptance as the most prominent architectonic appendage of the Hindu temple in the south.

106. The 7th century temple of Papanath at Pattadakal is the last of the temples in the Southern tradition to be crowned with a shikhara.

7. Plan of the Papanath temple Pattadakal. 1. Garbhagriha, 2. Pradakshina, 3. Mandapa.

## CHALUKYAS EVOLVE AN INTEGRATED PLAN

The Pallava craftsmen by concentrating their sculptural skills on the shape of the vimana alone, had undoubtedly evolved an elegant principal form for it. To them other functional elements of the temple like the "mandapa" (assembly hall) and entrance portico were mere ancillaries. They had not yet been able to integrate these into a balanced architectural whole. The Chalukyan artist, developing on the experience gained in organising disparate elements of the Lad Khan into the architectural entity of the temple of Badami displayed greater concern in evolving a logical overall architectural plan that would gather together the sanctum, mandapa and the entrance portico into a comprehensive planning entity. It is only natural then that a ground plan, reconciling the various components of the Hindu temple into an equable aggregate ultimately emerged in Chalukyan country. Under Vikramaditya I, the Chalukyans had established yet another capital city, that of Pattadakal, situated half way between the older cities of Badami and Aihole. The 7th century Papanath temple at Pattadakal, (Fig. 106), is the last example of a southern shrine adorned with a shikhara instead of the traditionally accepted vimana form. The craftsmen realised that the rather slender form of the shikhara could not substantially counterpoise the sprawling lower mass of the horizontality of their plan (Fig. 107). Moreover, the Dharamaraja Rath form of the Pallava sculptors of Mahabalipuram, had already won the enthusiastic approval of the priests and kings as the most appropriate temple spire profile.

## THE VIRUPAKSHA AT PATTADAKKAL

It the temple of Virupaksha, (Fig. 109), built at Pattadakkal, in the immediate neighbourhood of Papanath, the Chalukyan builder decided to surmount the garbhagriha with the more acceptable form of the southern vimana. In striking contrast to the Papanath, it at once presents an altogether substantial silhoutte. To achieve equable balance between the upper and the lower parts of the temple, a richly sculptured barrel-shaped form was projected out from the middle of the vimana to interlock as it were the tower and the mandapas. It effectively restrains too, the perceptible horizontal thrust of the mass below. The Mandapa for the first time is not treated merely as just another hall attached to the cella; rather a more convincing spatial link-up is established between the two by enveloping the dark square cella of the garbhagriha within the definable rectangular structure of the outer

108. The 740 A.D. Virupaksha temple at Pattadakal wherein the more substantial form of the vimana was installed over the garbhagriha.

**109.** Plan of the famous Virupaksha temple at Pattadakal.
1. Garbhagriha, 2. Pradakshina, 3. Mandapa.

walls of the mandapa (Fig. 108). The corridor like space along the back and the sides of the inner sanctum thus becomes a virtual pradkshina or circumambulatory path for the worshipper. He offers his momentary obeisance to the gods from a narrow ante-chamber like space between the opening to the cella and the clearly defined space of the mandapa. The mandapa in turn could be approached through any of the three porticos in the middle of its outer walls. As is apparent from the sum total, the superstructure of the temple is built up from a neatly synchronized ground plan.

## A TOUCH OF PALLAVA ELEGANCE

110. The 720 A.D. Vaikuntha Perumal at Kanchipuram with receding stories and pradakshina path's embodied in the mass of its vimana.

It was the Pallava craftsmen, once again, who added the necessary touch of elegance and perfection to the robust matter-of-fact architecture of the Chalukyas. The germs of the idea embodied in the Virupaksha temple are carried to their fruition in the Vaikunth Perumal temple (Fig. 112) in the ancient city of Kanchipuram. Here, the entrance portico of the mandapa are dispensed with and greater body was added to the mass of the cella by a pair instead of just one pradakshinapath. The diminishing form of the spire of the Vaikuntha Perumal is the only example of an Indian temple that infact makes functional use of the substantial mass embodied in the profile of the vimana. The vimana interior is actually designed as three distinct usable storeys, each with its own central shrine (Fig. 110). The two lower spires are surrounded by pradkshinapath's as well. The temple is virtually hugged by a colonnaded verandah a mere 8 feet (2.4

metres) away and consistently parallel to the mass of the outer walls of the main temple. The inner surface of the unpunctured walls of the surrounding verandah are adorned with a large as life freely composed sculptured frieze glorifying the origins and history of the Pallava kings (Fig. 111). The tightly knit plan, the intimate spaces, the multiple shrines, and the self glorifying Pallava sculpture suggest that the Vaikuntha Perumal was not a public shrine; rather it was the private family chapel of royalty, situated within or adjacent to the palace precinct.

111. The sculptured walls of the surrounding verandahs of the Vaikuntha Perumal glorifying the temporal powers of the day.

112. Part plan of the Vaikuntha Perumal temple at Kanchipuram, showing, 1. Garbhagirha, 2. Mandapa and 3. Pradakshina.

# STRUGGLES AND EMERGENCE OF THE RASHTRAKUTAS

The halcyon days of Pallava royalty however were to end soon. The Chalukya king Vikramaditya was smarting under the blow dealt to his father by the Pallavas and soon gained sufficient strength to attack the Pallava capital of Kanchipuram in 740 A.D. Though he succeeded in decimating the Pallavas, he is said to have spared the cities. This proved to be the last great test of strength between the Pallavas and the Chalukyas. Both the powers had exhausted their wealth and energies in incessant mutual wars. Rulers of other dynasties were quick to take advantage of the ensuing power vacuum in the southern peninsula.

The Cholas of the deeper south began gnawing at the remaining regions of Pallava power. The Rashtrakutas, the heirs of the earlier Vakatakas, had until now focussed their attention on the northern city of Kanauj. Now they found a rapidly weakening power on their southern flank. Doing a right about turn to suit the new situation, the Rashtrakutas quickly overcame the now feeble Chalukyan forces.

The heart of the new Rashtrakuta kingdom was the Western Ghats, a country side in which the rock-cut form of architecture had flourished for over 700 years, since the time the Buddhist monks had carved out the caves of Ajanta and Karli. It was not surprising therefore that the art be rejuvenated under the growing power of the Rashtrakutas. The revival got underway with the excavations of cave temples on the ancient island of Ghorapuri (modern Elephanta), just off the shores of modern Bombay.

112a. Plan of the great cave at Elephanta, near Bombay (780 A.D.).

113. The gigantic sculpture of the trimurti at Elephanta that is one of the great triumphs of the Indian sculptors' art.

## THE CAVES OF ELEPHANTA

In the closely clustered group of low hills, it was possible to carve out caves that were more like canopies of living rock hanging over generously lit spaces rather than mere tunnels of twilight run into the faces of cliffs as earlier caves had been. The mandapa which was approachable from three sides acquired a cruciform rather than rectangular plan of the earlier efforts at Badami, Ajanta and Mahabalipuram (Fig. 112a). The Mandapa is spaced out by columns to form aisles of varying widths. The planners were probably again imitating some structural timber model faithfully since such variations in the size of aisles were redundant in the fashioning of caves, freed as they were of the restraints of structural spans. The Indian carver avidly comprehending the sculptural potentialities of the dimly lit rear wall of the hall was in any case was not to be thwarted by the niceties of symmetrical planning. The enclosed shrine of Shiva, instead of being located in this more logical position at the rear of the hall, was placed instead in the middle of the entrance. This see-

mingly irrational choice is amply justified, when we look at the rear wall. It is brought to life by the famous titanic sculpture of the Trimoorti "looming out of the unknown depths of spaces and eternity" (Fig. 113). In fact it is obvious from the ponderous character of the massive columns, neither aligned to plumb nor accurately laid out to the right angle, that the accent in most Hindu cave temples was on creating surfaces for gigantic sculpture, rather than the spatial magic of Buddhist halls.

## THE GREAT KAILASA AT ELLORA

The scene now shifts to Elapura (now famous Ellora), near the Rashtrakuta capital of Kalkhed and only sixty miles from famous Ajanta. In the early phase, caves, that were mere variations of those at Badami or Elephanta, were added to the existing group of Buddhist caves. Architectonic power came into its own when the unrelenting rock cutter picked up once again the strains of the art of Pallava craftsmen of the Rathas of Mahabalipuram. The fullness of their dreams found expression under the patronage of the great Rashtrakuta king, Krishna I, when they contemplated the creation of the famous Kailasa temple at Ellora.

The Kailasa temple (Fig. 115) is a living rock replica of a structural form, larger than could ever have been constructed through the stone masonry technology of the 8th century. Once the idea of carving out a temple equal in area to the Parathenon and one and half times its height had been conceived, its production as well as evolution of design "became a matter of time, patience and skilled labour." That they were setting out on the herculean task of excavating some twenty million tonnes of rock, did not seem to deter the Indian stone carvers.

Their first step, though simple but laborious was to cut three massive trenches to isolate an "island" of rock over 200 feet (65.60 metres) long and 100 feet (32.80 metres) high from the oftworked cliff-like formations of Ellora. Beginning from the top, the rear mass of the island was gradually fashioned into the shape of a vimana to crown the main cell. Each portion of the carved rock was painstakingly finished and polished, before proceeding downwards to avoid erecting cumbersome scaffolding at a later stage.

The flat-roofed mandapa in front of the sanctum, seemingly supported on 16 columns in groups of four, the five shrines which surrounded the cella, and a pavilion housing a

**114.** A view of the great Kailasa, seen against the gigantic man made cliffside.

larger than life sacred Nandi bull, rest on a 25 feet (7.6 metres) high plinth (Fig. 116). Such a massive stylobate was obviously meant to lift the entire composition out of the yawning pit around. The Nandi Pavilion situated away from the main body of the stambhas reminiscent of the Asokan pillars in front of Buddhist chaitya hall of Karli are planted on either side of it. The fashioning of the front screen of natural rock into an entrance gateway completed the essentials of the main temple (Fig. 114).

To the untiring rock cutter, however, the craggy surfaces

115. Fifty million tonnes of rock were won with chisel and wedge to create the trench out of which loomed the once blazing white 800 A.D. temple of Kailasa at Ellora.

116. Platforms were formed at various levels to create a base for the sanctum, the mandapa and the Nandi pavilion.

that had been exposed from the surrounding cliffs, were a challenge in themselves. Into this scarp he tunneled a gallery, for circumambulating the temple and providing approaches to two subsidiary cave chapels carved out of the two sides. These in turn were at one time linked to the main temple by bridges which have now vanished.

In spite of its gigantic scale, to the builders the temple seemed as lost it does to the visitor today, against the immense backdrop of over-hanging cliffs of the same texture and hue as the shrine. In an effort to highlight its profile from the drabness of the surrounding pit, the stucco worker covered the entire surface of the Kailasa temple with a white gesso. When complete, it shone brightly, like the snow-capped peak of the Mount Kailasa in the Himalayas, the mythological earthly abode of the God Shiva. The sculptures on the plinth were at one time coated with a thin layer of poly-chromed plaster; no wonder, the Muslim invaders of the sixteenth century who saw it in its blazing glory referred to the temple as the "Rang Mahal" (the coloured palace).

That such a massive achievement as the Kailasa could ever be repeated, was inconceivable even to the legendary architect, responsible for its completion. He, it is said, admitted that "it could only be by magic that I could have constructed even this one." That magic truly was never repeated; the Kailasa was to be the great and glorious swan-song of rock architecture in India. Although the Jainas who won the patronage of the last Rashtrakuta king, also carved out cave temples of their faith at Ellora, including a mini-imitation of the Kailasa, there was nothing to equal the splendour and magnificence of the original.

In the ninth century, temples, apart from serving purely religious functions, were also becoming symbols of temporal power and the focus of urban social life. The rock cutters' art alas! by its very nature could be practised only in mountaineous and difficult rocky sites. Since the more prominent capital cities of the feudal times ware situated in the plains, the future of the art of rock carving was bleak. In giving to the rock-cut Kailasa the appearance of a splendid structural temple, the stone carver had, in a way, himself put the seal of doom on his own art. In its gigantic proportions alone, the Kailasa was like a gauntlet thrown at the stone mason, challenging him to create, if he could, edifices as lofty as the Kailasa. A challenge that, as we shall see, was taken up with great spirit to give rise to the great "temple-cathedrals" of medieval India.

# 13

## The Feudal North

### Temples in Rajasthan and Kashmir

RASHTRAKUTA power located as it was on the Deccan Plateau of Central India, overlooked the Southern regions as well as the plains of the North. It may well have subjugated the entire South, had the Rashtrakuta kings resisted the temptation of rising into a national power. Their political ambitions however proved larger and they continued to cast covetous glances at the city of Kanauj in the central plains. Thanks to King Harsha, Kanauj enjoyed the status that Pataliputra had under the Mauryas; the capture of this city was tantamount to paramountcy over northern India.

### THE RASHTRAKUTAS LOOK NORTHWARD

In trying to gain their objective, the Rashtrakutas had to con-

116 a. Map showing important sites of the medieval kingdoms of India, and left, ruins of the great 8th century Sun temple at Martand, Kashmir.

tend with the rising power of the Pratiharas in the west and the Palas of Bengal in the east. The Pratiharas (literally "door keepers") were probably a dynasty of palace officials risen to power. Their fighting strength had been mettled by successfully resisting pressures from the Arabs who had by the eighth century established large Muslim colonies in the Sind. The Palas, unknown until recently, had risen to prominence under the leadership of Gopala. King Gopala's armies soon prevailed in the traditionally rich area of Bengal and Bihar, and his kingdom had substantial commercial interests in Southeast Asia. It was, however, Gopala's son Dharampala who resolutely pitted Pala power against that of the Pratiharas and the Rashtrakutas for the conquest of Kanauj.

## THE LEGENDARY CITY OF KANAUJ

The three contestants turned out to be evenly matched in their war power. None was able to establish undisputed suzerainty over northern India, or even Kanauj. Paradoxically, in spite of—or more probably because of—being the cynosure of all eyes, including the Turks in the 10th century, the otherwise legendary city of Kanauj has not acquired any prominence in the known history of Indian architecture. It was so frequently sacked and demolished by warring armies that it is difficult to trace the remains even of any religious or secular ancient building of any consequence.

## RELIGIOUS FERVOUR AND FEUDALISM

From the time of the sack of Kanauj by the Turks, to the rise of Delhi 300 years later, no city enjoyed the status of being the political hub of the North. Instead a number of provincial capitals built to celebrate the short-lived splendour of their feudal overlords sprouted up all over the country. Apart from the inevitable fine differences in detail, similar social and political conditions seem to have prevailed in the various mini-kingdoms. Under the circumstances, it is confusing and often even reduntant, to describe the architecture of the north in the middle ages, in relationship to the ever changing temporal powers. Rather, it is more pertinent to understand that the euphemistic "religious fervour of the times" that gave rise no doubt to the building of thousands of temples all over the countryside was the result of an alliance—nay, almost conspiracy—between the ruling and priestly classes. The latter diverted the attention of the ever suffering commoner from his daily woes to promises of a blissful existence through the worship of the expanding Hindu pantheon. In return the ruling Kshatriya class paid exemplary tribute to the Brahmin, which really amounted to footing the bill for the performance of elaborate rituals and the building of great and many temples.

## TEMPLE BUILDING—THE ONLY PERMANENT ART

An architecturally consequential part of the deal seems to have been to agree to erect only religious edifices in permanent materials like stone. Secular architecture, including palaces for royalty, were assumed to be of a transitory second class nature and built in perishable materials like brick and timber. Thus, little secular architecture of the feudal period of any consequence has survived intact to date. And though, as we shall see, rules were propounded even for the "third class" architecture of houses for the common people these were obviously so humbly built, that not a trace is to be found of them except, of course, in the dictates of the Brahmins as contained in the ancient theological treatises on Hindu architecture described later. The perceivable history of Indian architecture of the middle ages continues therefore to be a story of the evolution of the art of temple building.

The conventional method of tracing the development of temple architecture in the north, has been to "treat its various phases not dynastically, but geographically so that each may be described according to the region in which it flourished." This, however, is to miss the point that throughout the development of the temple in the North, "there is an under-current of thought . . . which indicates that all these examples belong to the same wide movement." No doubt, craftsmen working in a particular region, evolved a distinct "school" of their own, yet they were often influenced by ideas developed in other regions.

The aim of this study being to trace the evolution of design of major forms of Indian architecture, it is often desirable —even necessary—to take liberties with the strictly regional classifications. The germ of an artistic vision often blossomed to perfection after cross breeding with the peculiar genius of other regions. For our purposes, therefore, it is inevitable that we hop from place to place and style to style to see how the shape of the Shikhara, or the Vimana or the Mandapa or the Garbhagriha was moulded into endless number of variations by the ingenuity of the various schools of craftsmen working in the far flung corners of northern India.

## TEMPLES OF OSIAN

To pick up the strains once again one finds that the earliest subsistent link in the evolution of the Shikhara, the birth of which, during the heyday of the Gupta empire, has already been described in detail, is to be found in the village of Osian near modern Jodhpur in Rajasthan. In the eighth century, it was probably the capital of the Pratiharas and "is an example not uncommon in India of a considerable city, whose substance has departed and only the spirit remains"—the spirit being a handful of small but elegant temples crafted not in the familiar brick masonry of the Guptas, but in everlasting stone.

The shikhara that had become the crowning feature of the sixth century Hindu shrine of Deogarh, was now adapted into the design of a full fledged Osian temple such as the one classified as "temple No. 2." To the cella and Shikhara of their prototype the builders of Osian added a Mandapa or open assembly hall supported on columns (Fig. 117). The edifice is raised on a high plinth, the outer surface adorned with the

117. The Deogarh type shikhara is adapted into the so-called temple no. 2 at Osian, consisting of a mandapa on slender columns and with a sloping stone bench.

118. A more perfect example of the Osian group of temple is the Surya temple of 900 A.D.

119. Plan of the temple of Surya at Osian, showing 1. Garbhagriha and 2. Mandapa.

rich plasticity of the sculpture of the Gupta period. In grafting the Shikhara into a comprehensive temple design the false porticos of the Deogarh example were found to be redundant. This omission of a classical idiom is more than amply compensated by the retention of a few rich folk elements. The sloping stone seat of the Lad Khana type now exquisitely decorated, surrounds the Mandapa. Also the plinth of the temple is stopped short of the end portico columns, which are carried right down to the natural ground adding to their slenderness (Fig. 118). Perhaps unintentionally, the builders introduced a flair that matured into a classic form in a subsequent temple at Osia, that of Surya (the Sun god).

In the Surya temple (Fig. 119) the Shikhara, instead of being a slender tapering form, acquires more body and rises up in a single, more confident curve towards a disc-like Kalasa stone capping the apex. The mandapa too is equally dignified. Shedding some of its folk trappings it emerges as a rectangular hall with its flat roof held up over rows of stately square columns rising up from a substantial plinth. The slenderness of the columns of the entrance portico, which rise straight up from ground level, is emphasised by vertical flutings on their circular shafts. The temple was at one time set within a rectangular precinct defined by a cloister, at each corner of which was located a subsidiary shrine.

# HINDU TEMPLES IN THE VALLEY OF KASHMIR

Development of the Hindu temple along parallel lines was continuing in other urban centres of the plains. Let us, however, also have a look at the contemporary styles developing in the more isolated hill states such as Nepal, Kashmir and Garhwal. The distinctive architecture of these regions was more suited to their geographic and climatic conditions, and even absorbed traits from the styles of neighbouring nations. The most flourishing of the hill states that falls into this purview, is that of the fabled valley of Kashmir. In the sixth century A.D., the Buddhists who had fled from the wrath of the Huns, had built a number of monasteries in Kashmir. The climate being none too kind to brick masonry, not one of these has survived in a recognizable architectural form. In the eighth century, Kashmir was under the rule of King Lalitaditya who had developed it into a prosperous and virtually self-sufficient state. The ambitions of the Hindu King Lalitaditya, however, were not entirely restricted to the valley. He made several successful forays south into the plains and was also partly responsible for warding off the threat posed by Arab expansionism in the Sind. By opening up channels with the plains, Lalitaditya exposed the valley to the influence of Hinduism, which ultimately prevailed over Buddhism. The craftsmen of Kashmir, though, were not a part of the stream of architectural development in the plains. With their background of Buddhist artistic traditions, they evolved a style of Hindu temple architecture, with a distinct flavour of its own.

120. Plan of the Sankaracharya temple at Srinagar.

The earliest known Hindu temple, that of Shankaracharya, (Fig. 121) is located on a hill top overlooking the famous Dal Lake of modern Srinagar. Built in the eighth century on an octagonal platform, it is approached by an imposing flight of steps and has an unusual plan. Though from outside, the shrine appears to be the conventional square in plan (Fig. 120) with recessed chases running along its periphery, it encloses in fact a circular cella, echoing the shape of the rounded Shiva Lingam installed in it. What distinguishes the temple visually from its prototype of the plains though, is the entrance portico. This is in the form of a stone abutment to the entrance doorway of the cella and contains a triple cusped trefoil arch, set inside a high pitched triangulated pediment. The trefoil arch is obviously derived from the Buddhist Chaitya arch, with modifications effected by the Greco-Roman traditions of Gandhara craftsmen. The triangular pediment, however, could have been derived either from the gable end of the

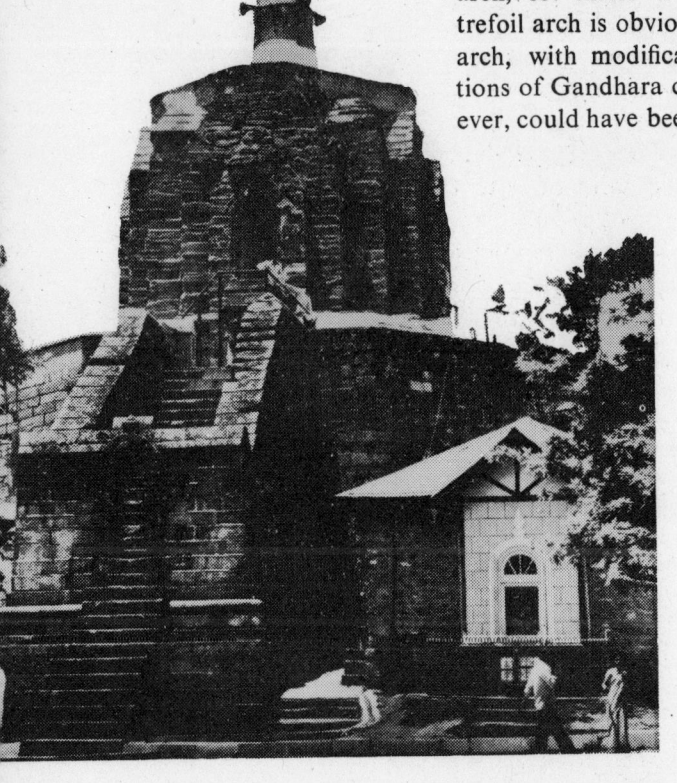

121. The Sankaracharya at Srinagar like many other living shrines has suffered due to various unplanned architectural modifications. At one time, it must have been an imposing edifice.

pitched timber roofs common in the hill country around the valley or is an ungainly steep derivation of the classical Greek pediment, well known to the Gandhara builders. The tower that crowns the cella instead of being the curvilinear Shikhara is a plain unornamented pyramid. Its smooth sloping surfaces do not make for a very attractive form but are eminently suited to ward off the winter snows, just like the timber steeples of the shrines of the hillside hamlets.

A distinguished, but modest, shrine like the Shankaracharya, was, however, hardly likely to satisfy the growing ambitions of the Kashmir kings. Commanded to build more elaborate and glorious shrines, the local architects instinctively turned to Buddhist prototypes for inspiration. This is evident from the famous Sun Temple of Martand (Fig. 116 a) and the temple of Avantipur which are laid out much like the great Stupa courts of Takhte-Bahi and Takht-e-Jamshed, built in the Gandhara country over 400 years ago.

## HILL CONSTRUCTION TECHNIQUES

A word must be said here about the techniques of construction employed by the hill craftsmen. The 8th century builders of Kashmir were way ahead of their contemporaries of the plains and peninsular India. While the Hindu mason of the plains was content to build his temples with stone masonry laid dry, the walls of the temples of Kashmir were constructed of evenly dressed ashlar masonry, carefully jointed together either with lime mortar or even steel dowels; techniques that may well have been learnt from the craftsmen of neighbouring western regions. However, as we have seen even these refined techniques could not stand up to the rigorous climate of the region and only a few of the vast number of temples that must have been built have survived (Fig. 122).

122. Plan and elevation of a typical small countryside Hindu shrine showing the hill construction techniques typical of Kashmir.

**123.** Plan of the 9th century Avanti Swami temple near Srinagar. 1. Sanctum, 2. Peristyle and 3. Entrance portico.

Lalitaditya's successor, King Avantivarman, heralded the beginning of his rule by laying out a new capital city—that of Avantipur, overlooking a bend in the Jhelum, 18 miles south-east of modern Srinagar. Its chief attraction must have been the Avanti Swami Temple which if anything is in an even worse state of preservation than its prototype, the Sun temple at Martand.

At one time, however, the Avanti Swami temple (Fig. 123) possessed the necessary wherewithal for the performance of elaborate Hindu rituals, including a ceremonial bathing tank, a kirti stambha or heraldic pillar and subsidiary shrines in each corner of the court (Fig. 124). In its heyday it must have presented a stately picture of the classical panchratana type of temple plan. Its architectural character however had not evolved much beyond that of Martanda.

124. A conjectural restoration of the Avanti Swami temple as it must have been during the regime of King Lalitaditya in Kashmir.

125a. Plan of the great Sun temple at Martand. 1. Sanctum, 2. Peristyle and 3. Entrance portico.

## THE SUN TEMPLE MARTAND

Martand, victim both of the harsh climate as well as the ultimate decline of Hindu power in Kashmir, today is a heap of uncared for ruins (Fig. 123). It is nevertheless evident that in its design, the plan of the Buddhist monastery has been adapted to create a new form for the Kashmiri Hindu temple. The central place of the sacred stupa is taken up by a shrine of the Shankaracharya type. The form of the trefoil arch abuttment that was the entrance to the Shankaracharya has been added on all the four sides, and the temple is set on a high square platform. The perfectly symmetrical design also reminds one of the temple of Deogarh. What were cells for the residence of monks in the Buddhist monastery are transmuted into so many niches, adorned with quasi-Doric columns and filled with images of the unending pantheon of Hindu deities. The entrance pylon to the rectangular courtyard defined by the niches, is in its architectonics a replica of the central shrine.

**125b.** The impressive remains of the great Sun temple at Martand.

# 14

# Rajput "Vanshas" and the Kalinga Kings

## Classicism at Gwalior and Bhubaneswar

LEAVING Kashmir, which rose again to architectural prominence only under the Great Moghuls more than 500 years later, we come down once again to the plains. The Hindu mason in spite of his rather rudimentary structural techniques, was busy erecting temples for his proliferating overlords. The fluxionary state of eighth century feudal India, gave rise to many centres of feverish building activity. The most prominent of these were located in the central region of the hills surrounding Gwalior, the western plains of Gujarat and Kathiawar, the eastern coast of Orissa and in the desert strongholds of Rajasthan in the north-west.

### TELI-KA-MANDIR AT GWALIOR

While Gujarat, as we shall see later, took its cue from the neighbouring style of the temples of Osian, the so called Teli-Ka-Mandir (literally Oil Man's temple) within the hill top fort of Gwalior is in a class by itself. Local legend attributes its peculiar name to the fact that it was built from the donations given by an oil merchant. Judging from its style, it is more probable that the name is a distortion of Telengana (modern Andhra) suggesting that it was designed by an architect from that region. In fact, it was the last grand attempt at adopting the Buddhist Chaitya hall roof over a rectangular plan (Fig. 126) as a model for a Hindu shrine. One will recall that this was one of the seven forms of the Rathas carved out at Mahabalipuram in the south. The pile of masonry of the

126. Plan of the Teli-ka-Mandir above and left a view of Bhubaneswar, the legendary city of a thousand temples.

127. The 24 metre high tower of the Teli-ka-Mandir (800 A.D.). One of the few examples of a northern Hindu temple adorned with a Buddhist Chaitya hall type roof.

Teli-Ka-Mandir (Fig. 127) with richly sculptured horizontal friezes, towers 80 feet (24.3 metres) into the sky. Half way up, the rectangular prism of the base becomes a pyramid, crowned by the hump of the barrel vaulted roof form so popular with the Buddhist architect. Though a form discarded by the northern Hindu architect, a variation of it, as we shall see, was destined to dot the southern skyline in the form of massive ceremonial gateways of its myriads of temples.

## THE VANSHAS

The desert region of Rajasthan in the middle ages, was peopled by martial clans, the forefathers of the modern Rajput. The foremost of these were the Parihars, Chauhans, Parmars and Solankis. They were the descendants of warlike tribes who were forced to proliferate into the desert region of India, under the pressure of the Hun invasions of the north-west region in the fourth century A.D. They had by now persuaded the Brahmin keepers of the Puranas (traditional records and stories of Hindu geneologies) to accord them not only Kshatriya warrior status within the caste system, but also geneaologies, claiming their descent from legendary Solar and Lunar races, the popular Suryavanshi and Chandravanshi. The social status even of the modern proud Rajput is based on his belonging to either of these major "Vanshas".

## THE SURAJ KUND, DELHI

The Tomars, an offshoot of the Rajput Chauhans, had in 736 A.D. founded the city of Dhillika (modern Delhi) on the banks of the Jamuna river. It is said to have contained more than 20 temples of the Hindu and Jaina faith. Subsequently in the 11th century building material salvaged from most of these was absorbed into the Muslim architecture of Delhi. That the Tomar craftsmen had reached a high level of temple building is testified even by the ruinous remains of the so called Suraj Kund in the south of Delhi (Fig. 128). This at one time must have been a massive temple, probably dedicated to the Sun God, overlooking a large circular ritual bathing tank. Today only the tank remains, that too in a ruinous state, the main shrine having completely vanished. A similar fate seems to have overtaken the creation of the Paramar Kings in the central Indian region of Malwa, which too was ultimately devastated by the Muslims.

128. Ruins of the platform and tank of the 8th century Suraj Kund near Delhi, where at one time stood a temple dedicated to the Sun God.

# THE ETERNALLY HOLY KALINGA

Of the other states, the land of Kalinga (modern Orissa) the conquest of which had been the turning point of Asoka's career, was coming into the limelight once again. It was not only one of the major spring-boards for the spread of Indian culture to the far east, but was also emerging as a flourishing centre of temple building activity.

The temporal history of this region, like that of most of India at the time is vague and obscure. The little that is known suggests that Kalinga, in the true feudal tradition, was ruled by a succession of kings, who sought personal glorification, through the building of temples rather than empires or cities. Orissa is yet another of the many examples of the crafty collusion whereby the King and Priest ruled over a "people (that) were quite content to live in hovels and mean habitations themselves, but for the houses of the gods, they would not stint either expenditure or labour." The cities of Kalinga then are, not surprisingly, more renowned for their intensely devotional fervour and great temples than civil architecture, devoid as they are of any semblance of town planning. Over a period of seven hundred years, the holiest of the holies, the city of Bhubaneshwar came to acquire some seven thousand temples and little else.

## VAITAL DEUL AT BHUBANESHWAR

Early experiments in temple building were as ever made with forms derived from Buddhist architecture, as in the seventh century—Vaital Deul temple at Bhubaneshwar (Fig.129). The 35 feet (10.6 metres) high "deul" or shrine of this temple is in fact a refined version of the Teli-Ka-Mandir at Gwalior described earlier. Like the latter, this too is surmounted by a roof form of unmistakable Buddhist ancestry, the familiar Chaitya hall vault. The similarity however ends here since the Orissa craftsmen grafted many original elements into his design. For example, he chose to leave unadorned the outer surface of the vault and instead planted three Kalasa type finals, generally found over a shikhara, on the ridge of the lower vault. What is more the form of the familiar north-Indian shikhara is attached to the corners of the otherwise undistinguished rectangular flat roofed mandapa in front (Fig. 131). The rather incongruous introductions of the shikhara even as a subsequent element into the design, indicated the general trend of the Orissa builder, towards favouring the shikhara as a more

**129.** Another attempt to adopt the Buddhist medium to a Hindu temple-the Vaital Deul temple at Bhubaneswar (850 A.D.).

**131.** The Vaital Deul at Bhubaneswar showing shikharas, at the four corners.

**130.** The typical "shoulder shaped" Orissa shikhara.

acceptable finial for the Hindu temple. However, ignoring the pronounced elliptic curve of the shikhara of the Gupta period for ease of construction, the Orissa craftsman chose to interpret the Shikhara as an almost perpendicular prismatic tower. The vertical profile of the Orissa shikhara converged only near the apex, towards the circular Kalasa or crowning stone at the top. This socalled "shoulder type" spire (Fig. 130) became in due course the distinguished feature of Orissa temples. Simple shrines consisting of a small "Sri Mandir", or "deul" as the main cella is called, crowned by the typical Orissa are Shikhara, grouped all over the Orissa countryside much like wayside Buddhist stupas, in Asoka's time.

132. The Parasurameswara temple showing shrine and mandapa, 800 A.D.

## A MANDAPA FOR THE DEUL

Inevitably, the need was soon felt for attaching a Mandapa or covered hall to single roomed shrines wherein worshippers could congregate and sing devotional hymns to the enshrined deity. For this purpose often an existing simple shrine would be expanded. In the eighth century temple of Parasurameswar, (Fig. 132) the earliest known example of such a modification, an extremely ponderous lowslung structure was attached to the Sri Mandir of an earlier period. Rectangular in plan, (Fig. 133) the central aisle of the mandapa along its longer side is flat roofed. The side aisles are covered with massive stone slabs laid to slope, leaving between the two roofs a narrow horizontal opening forming a sort of clerestorey lighting of the interior. The walls are made of cumbersome almost cycloplean blocks of stone, the openings within being more appropriate for pygmies. In structural techniques the entire effort is not much advanced from the rather primitive achievements of the seventh century temple builders of Aihole.

133. Plan of the Parasurameswara temple showing. 1. Garbhagriha, and 2. Mandapa.

## THE LITTLE GEM OF MUKTESWAR

Once an enlarged temple including the mandapa became customary, a more elegant edifice such as the temple of Mukteswar (Fig. 134) also at Bhubaneshwar emerged. So far in Orissan architecture the mandapa had been treated merely as a room, somehow or the other appended to the door of the main shrine. We have seen how at Aihole, Osian and the early Orissan temples, it remained rather incongruous and uncertain both in design and construction. Now for the first time, the mandapa received due attention from its designer. Almost instinctively it would seem the Hindu architect's first act was to make it square rather than rectangular in plan. He then proceeded to roof it with a tapering form but realising the

134. Plan of the Mukteswara temple at Bhubaneswar showing 1. Garbhagriha and 2. Mandapa.

145

135. The bamboo purlins of the rural form became the triangular stone uprights of the series of deep cornices that are the pyramidical roof of the Orissa mandapa.

subservience of the mandapa to the "deul", he designed it as a shallow pyramid substantially lower than the Shikhara tower. It was constructed as a series of corbelled courses of stone, which appear externally as cornices punctuated by small triangular uprights (Fig. 135). In doing so, the craftsmen as ever, were drawing their inspiration from rural forms. The uprights are nothing but a geometric crystallisation of the bamboo purlins of the thatch original. Each cornice seems to sail over the lower one; an illusion created by a marked and well shaded gap between two consecutive courses. The inspired hand that devised the form of the mandapa also gave clear definition to the temple tower. Each horizontal course of the shoulder type shikhara is well modulated and defined. Entrance to the temple compound is gained through a kind of torana, consisting of two vertical pillars spanned by a corbelled though semicircular richly sculptured arch, an elegant element that does not appear again in the temples of Orissa.

The precincts of the Mukteswar temple are defined by a low parapet adorned with lands of richly sculptured friezes. The richness of form, the meticulous planning of both the Deul and Jagmohan, (Fig. 136) under the guiding hand of an anonymous Orissan master architect resulted in a little gem the like of which was never repeated; not at least in the land of Kalinga.

Almost all other temples, of even the 9th and 10th century of the Orissa style display an inherent weakness in establishing an appropriate relationship between the cella and the mandapas. The shortcoming may be attributed to the fact that rarely did the Orissa architect get a chance to visualise his temple as a single entity. In his almost two centuries of building in Orissa he was more commissioned to add to existing shrine, rather than to design and execute complete new temples. In the process he seems to have lost the capacity to knit together the elements of his creations into a crystalline architectural statement. For such a crystallization, we must look elsewhere; to an even more famous centre of "religious fervour," that of Khajuraho.

136. A rare Orissa example of a temple planned and built without subsequent additions—the little gem of Mukteswara at Bhubaneswar (900 A.D.).

# 15

# The Chandelas of Bundel- khand

## Khajuraho's Jagadambi and Puri's Jagannath

A parallel development, the essence of which was to permeate later even into Orissa, was taking place over 500 miles north-west in the Bundelkhand region of central India. Here the Chandelas, an offshoot of one of the Rajput martial clans, had gained supremacy in about 1000 A.D. Their building craftsmen had gained sufficient practical experience in construction by skillful engineering of large civil works, such as reservoirs and tanks. With equal skill, their colleagues proceeded to embellish the capital city of Khajuraho with temples both of the Hindu and Jain faiths (Fig. 137).

The architects of the Chandelas appear to have been well aware of the visual shortcomings of the temples of Orissa. Even their earliest efforts display a total comprehension of temple design that had eluded the builder of Orissa for a couple of hundred years. Probably the physical proximity of Khajuraho to Orissa and Gujarat where the nucleus of such a design had already emerged also helped the Chandella builders. The largest group of their temples is set in the now desolate and sleepy village of Khajuraho. What at one time was probably the bustling capital of a burgeoning dynasty, is today but a cluster of 16 deserted temples. Only in one of these is the deity still worshipped. The rest are a tourist haunt, world famous for their architectural excellence as well as the profusion of erotic sculpture.

## THE EARLY TEMPLES OF KHAJURAHO

All the temples of Khajuraho are set on broad high terraces. They were probably "disposed rather unsymmetrically around the borders of an ornamental sheet of water" which today is the rather sterile though well tended gardens of the Archaelogical Survey of India. Though the platforms of the temples were sufficiently elevated above the water level, the floor level of most of them is raised by yet another 10 to 12 feet (3 to 3.6 metres). This gave the builder the opportunity to erect stately flight of steps leading from the terrace to the entrance. Over this the plan of the temple is laid out, not as a series of "conjoined buildings but as a compact architectural synthesis" (Fig. 139).

Even one of the comparatively small temples like the Lakshmana (Fig. 138) displays a remarkable unity of composition. The cella, the mandapa and the entrance vestibule are the parts of a harmonious whole. A narrow pillared aisle with stone benches on either side stretches out to receive the visitor at the top of the flight of steps from the terrace below.

137. Plan of the Lakshamana temple at Khajuraho consisting of 1. Garbhagriha, 2. Antrayla, 3. Mandapa and 4. Ardha mandapa.

138. The graceful outline of the Vishwanatha at Khajuraho temple (1000 A.D.).

Passing through an open mandapa supported on four central columns, he approaches the anteroom or "antralaya" immediately behind which lies the dark cubic cella. An elegant skyline of the body of the temple was only a logical outcome of such a precisely delineated plan. The apex of the shallow pyramidical roofs over the front compartments ascend gracefully towards the climax of the shikhara rising over the cella of the garbhagriha.

139. Plan of the Vishwanatha temple at Khajuraho, showing 1. Garbhagriha, 2. Mandapa, 3. Ardha mandapa and 4. Pradakshina.

140. An early Khajuraho shikhara.

141, 142, 143. Urusringa upon Urusringa. The development of the glorious shikharas of Khajuraho.

## THE SHIKHARAS OF KHAJURAHO

The shikharas of Khajuraho are architectural masterpieces in their own right. Gone is the rigid verticality of the Orissa Shikhara. Instead we find here an ascending parabolic outline rising to the top in one graceful sweep (Fig. 140). Gone too is the tier upon tier of stone courses that tended to compromise the impact of height in the Orissa shikhara. On the contrary and almost defiantly it would seem, the Chandela builders concealed the inevitable horizontal joints of the courses of masonry, under clearly defined projecting vertical bands planted in the middle of each of the four faces of the shikhara, which rose up towards the Amalaka or capstone, in perfect rhythm with the curvilinear outline of the shikhara (Fig. 141). This however was only the bare bone of a complex ornamental system that the builders devised for their temple spires.

It was now clear in their mind that the shikhara, soaring high into the skies was going to be the crowning glory of their scheme. Would the rather bare parabolic profile of the shikhara bands be effective enough for the purpose? The blank surfaces of the vertical bands attached to the body brought up in the Hindu sculptor his inherent sense of "horror vacuum". By now, the Hindu sculptor had acquired the techniques of being able to create visual drama within the parameters of discipline rather than mere gimmickry. He, therefore, devised the simple but appealing idea of ornamenting the body of the monumental form of his Shikhara with vari-dimensional aspects of its own shape. Thus, Shikharas in semi-relief, complete with the amalka and kalasa (Urusringa, in Hindu terminology) were applied over the four upper surfaces of the body of the shikhara (Fig. 142). This application, he discovered, imparted an extraordinarily smooth sweep to the soaring profile of the spire. Assured by his initial success, the builder had little hesitation in repeating the technique ad-infinitum. With gay abandon he proceeded to plant shikhara over shikhara on the main body wherever he appropriately could. Thus, the corners of the base of the tower became like a vertical chain of superimposed full bodied mini-shikharas. The body of the tower was filled out and its gracefully ascending profile further enhanced by superimposed gradually ascending Urusringa upon Urusringa on the four faces.

The silhouette of a Khajuraho composition, captures in all its magnificence the impression of a line of lofty mountain ranges (Fig. 145). The functional part of the temple, the cella and its attached mandapas, are in contrast strikingly modest in volume. They are dimly lit spaces not unlike a cave carved out from the body of an artificially created mountain (Fig. 145). Psychologically, the Indian builder was resolved to preserve the ancient traditional spirit of an Indian place of worship as a mysterious and dark cave, excavated out of living rock. In Khajuraho, he came as magnificently close to achieving this concept in reality, as a man-made structure ever could.

144, 145. A sectional elevation of a Khajuraho temple, showing the similarity of the profile to a range of lofty mountains.

146. The great Lingaraja at Bhubaneswar (1000 A.D)

## ORISSA—A STUDY IN CONTRAST

Returning once again to the contemporary development taking place in Orissa in the mid 11th century we find builders involved in the process of adding gargantuan structures to the now thriving pilgrimage centres of Bhubaneshwar, and the coastal holy town of Puri. Stylistically they clung to structures built over massive masonry walls with minimal openings. They were unable to emulate the Khajuraho example of

airy open mandapas, with their huge pyramidical roofs seemingly delicately poised over a cluster of stone pillars. One of the more ambitious efforts of this period are the great Lingaraja temples at Bhubaneshwar (Fig. 146) and the famous Jagannath temple at Puri, both of which are almost identical in style and construction.

## THE GREAT LINGARAJA

The Lingaraja, initially, consisted only of a cella and a mandapa each, of truly gigantic proportions. The cella alone is 56 feet (17 metres) square (Fig. 148) and rises about 140 feet (43 metres) into the sky. The mandapa is rectangular in plan large enough to require additional support in the form of four massive central columns and its pyramidical roof reaches a height of almost a 100 feet (30.4 metres).

Unlike the temples of Khajuraho which were completely deserted after the fall of the Chandelas, those of Orissa, particularly the larger ones like the Lingaraja developed into important centres of Hindu pilgrimage and the elaborate ritual of Hindu worship is carried out in them to date. The Brahmin system of worship was becoming increasingly complex. It was no longer sufficient merely to obtain *darshan* or propitiate the gods by obsequeity or merely sing hymns in his praise. The

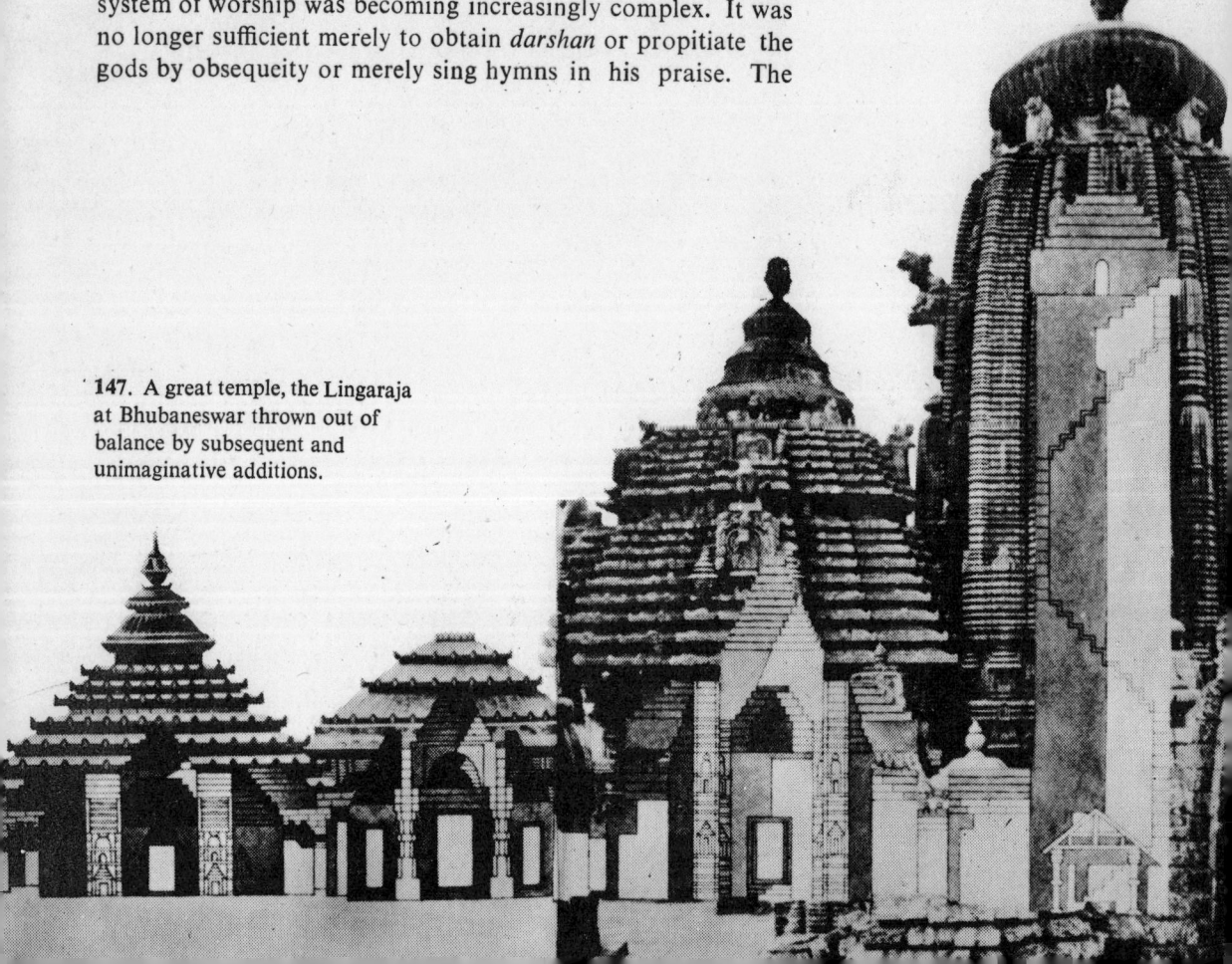

147. A great temple, the Lingaraja at Bhubaneswar thrown out of balance by subsequent and unimaginative additions.

148. Plan of the great Lingaraja at Bhubaneswar. 1. Sri Mandir, 2. Jagmohan, 3. Nat Mandir and 4. Bhog Mandir.

concept of the temple as "House of God" was carried to its almost childish extreme. The Brahmins made it mandatory to feed, clothe, bathe and entertain the sculptured image of the deity, as if God personified was himself installed in the sanctum. The Brahmins now became the self-appointed trustees of this house, and the worshippers, the wilful servants of their idiosyncrasies.

In order that the various new rituals be carried out with due pomp and glory, two more halls had to be added to the existing mandapa or "Jagmohan" (in Orissan terminology) of the Lingaraja. In the temples of Orissa these were called the Nat Mandir, where devadasis (literally—female servants of the gods) danced, ostensibly to entertain the gods but more likely to soothe the carnal desire of the Brahmins. In the Bhog Mandir which was the next hall, food received from the houses of rich donors was supposedly blessed by the Holy presence and a substantial part of it distributed to the poor. The image of God, enshrined in the inner sanctum, could look out upon the world only through one opening, that in the direction of the Jagmohan. Thus inevitably, for due fulfilment of the ritual of entertainment and blessing, the Nat Mandir and Bhog Mandir, could be attached only along the existing Deul-Jagmohan axis. The square additional halls, not unlike the Jagmohan in plan, elevation and methods of construction added no doubt to the volumetric prominence of the Lingaraja temple but not to its architectural composition. The subsequent additions, being taller than the original Jagmohan, threw the entire composition out of balance (Fig. 147). The silhouette, unlike the gradually descending sweep of the Khajuraho temple became rather awkwardly convex since the Bhog and Nat Mandir soared higher into the sky than the Jagmohan planted in the middle.

Looking at the myriads of other Orissan temples it would seem as if the craftsmen in spite of years of experience could visualise the temple only as a mere sum total of a series of unrelated units. The 12th century Anant Vasudev temple is one of the rare examples of an Orissan temple conceived and executed in toto. Though its silhouette has a clearly ascending profile, is it still as rigidly uncomprising as so many sergeant majors standing in drill (Fig.149) in sharp contrast to the fluid lines of a group of dancers that the temples of Khajuraho are. The temple though smaller than its better known predecessors, the Lingaraj and Jagan Nath, stands on a more substantial plinth quite likely suggested by the massive stylobates of the shrines of Khajuraho.

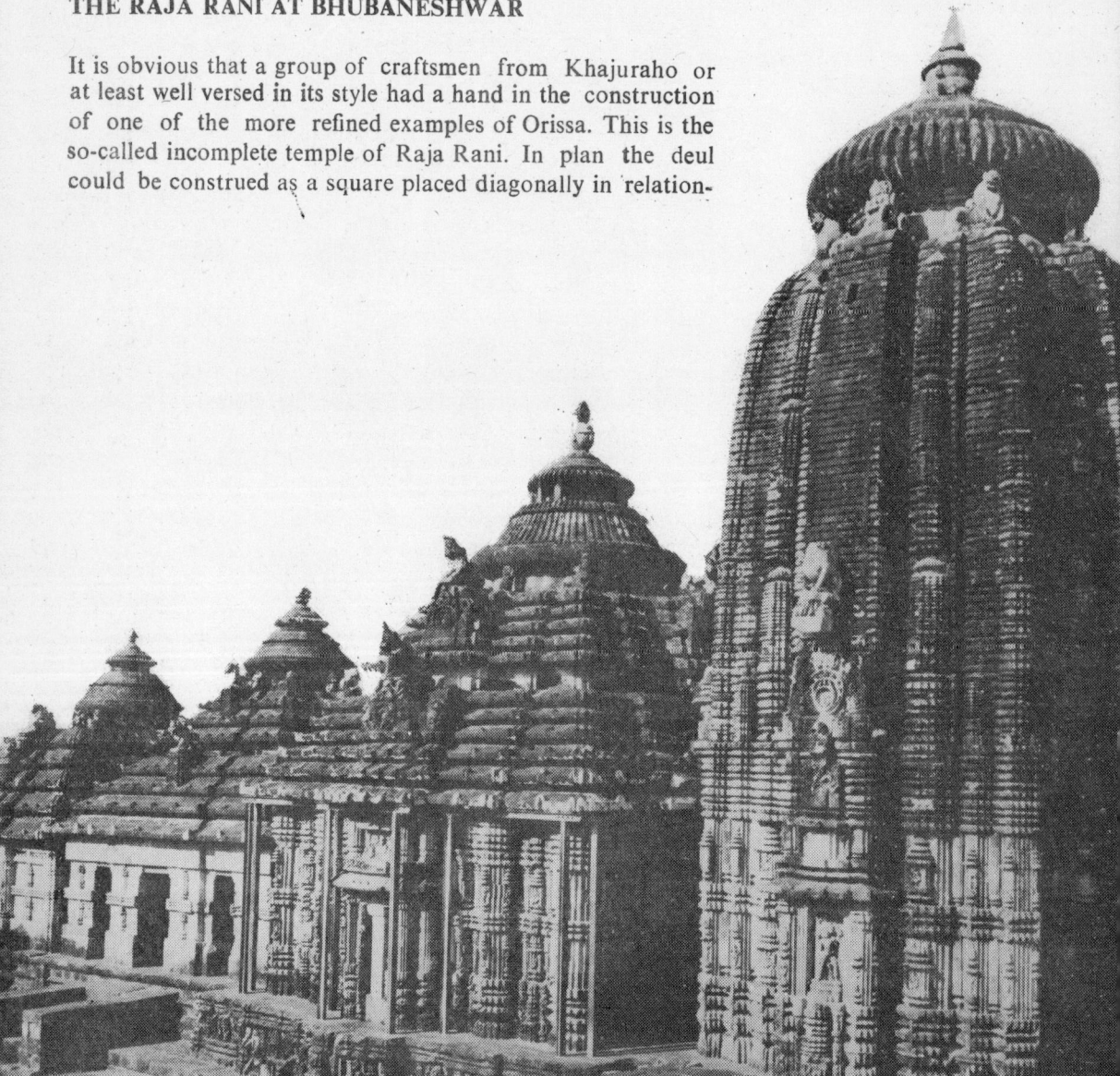

**149.** The 12th century Ananta Vasudeva temple at Bhubaneswar.

## THE RAJA RANI AT BHUBANESHWAR

It is obvious that a group of craftsmen from Khajuraho or at least well versed in its style had a hand in the construction of one of the more refined examples of Orissa. This is the so-called incomplete temple of Raja Rani. In plan the deul could be construed as a square placed diagonally in relationship to the Jagmohan with one of its corners rather than the broad face, forming the link with the Jagmohan (Fig.150). In its elevational effect the Khajuraho device of attached shikhara quoins and urusringas is used to good effect. Though the temple spire acquired a pronounced sense of cambered grace and verticality, it still looks rather stiff and lacks the feline rhythm of its Khajuraho prototype (Fig. 151). Hereafter, the only major remaining example of the Orissa craftsman's art is the great 13th century Sun temple of Konarak. This is discussed in a later chapter, in its relationship to the great masterpieces of other regional styles, such as the Kandarya Mahadeo of Khajuraho and the Sun Temple of Modhera in Gujarat.

150. The diagonally oriented plan of the Rajrani temple at Bhubaneswar showing 1. Deul and 2. Jagmohan.

151. Shikhara of the 10th century Orissa temple of Raj Rani inspired by the form of the Shikharas of Khajuraho.

# 16

# The Hindu Jaina Axis of Gujarat

## "Mandapa" temples in the West

WE turn then to the western region of India, comprising parts of modern Gujarat, Kathiawar, Rajasthan and central India. This area was under the stable rule of the Solanki dynasty that had its capital at Anhilwad Pattan (near modern Ahmedabad). By dint of its location it controlled a long and jagged coast-line abounding with natural harbours. Consequently, it was the focus of great trading activity between the eastern and western worlds, which led to the growth of a prosperous and flourishing mercantile community. The astute Brahmin was not to be left out of the general prosperity. Through the holding of "a great assembly on market day" he was able to persuade the rich community "to an agreement to set apart for the gods certain taxes. The shopkeepers were to give a spoonful of every kind of grain that was sold, while of cotton, each shop was to give as much as a man could hold in his hand"... and so on.

### INVASIONS AND EARTHQUAKES

With this abundance of funds, and an artistic heritage going back to the time of the Guptas, the western country at one time was studded with fine examples of the building art. Possessed as these temples were of almost legendary wealth, they later became the target of the raids of Muslim adventurers. The most prominent of these raiders was Mahmud of Ghazni who attacked the area frequently in the early 11th century. Among the many temples that he sacked the richest and most famous was that of Somnath at Veraval on the Kathiawar coast. Subsequently, in the early 19th century a devastating earthquake, with its epicentre somewhere in Kathiawar, reduced many religious edifices that were "splendours of sculptured stone" to "crumbling piles of broken and shapeless masonry." The few temples that have survived both the natural and man-made catastrophies are at Kiradu, Ghumli, Modhera and Sejakpur. It is evident even from these fragmentary remains that the Gujarat craftsman's peculiar genius lay in the building of sometimes exquisite, and sometime elaborate and grandiose "mandapas" for his temples.

### THE TEMPLES OF KIRADU

This propensity for designing the mandapa with exquisite care is noticeable even in the early temple of Somesvara (Fig. 152) that stands today in a ruinous condition in the deserted village of Kiradu in modern Rajasthan. The tower over the Garbh-

151a. The stern and forbidding Mahavira, the Jaina.

griha is a rather ungainly pile of miniature shikhara shaped turrets and triangular pedimented niches, erected over a richly though incohesively sculptured base. The mandapa is composed altogether more competently. Unhampered by an enclosing wall, it is an open structure held up on a series of columns (Fig. 153). The arrangement of these is a departure from the traditional pattern of columns fixed along a rectangular or square grid. The heart of the mandapa is an octagonal space defined by eight tall and slender columns. Four aisles radiate out from the central octagon; three terminate in entry points to the mandapa and one leads to the garbhagriha. The plan is completed by setting the entire arrangement within a diagonally sited square, the four outer sides of which are further enriched by a series of rectangular offsets. The taller columns on the periphery of the central octagon are tied to-

152, 153. The pile up of mini-shikhara turrets that is the shikhara of the Someswara at Kiradu and the remains of a once glorious open pillared manadapa.

gether by stone lintels and provide an intermediate ring of support for the pyramidical roof, constructed as ever by concentric rings of corbelled stone work. The zigzag outline of the mandapa creates not only "vivid passage of light and shade" but also provides ideal oblong surfaces for embellishing with sculpture. The familiar inclined "Asana" or stone bench that forms a heavy sloping band of stone over and all along the mass of the plinth reduces the appearance of the peripheral supports to mere dwarf columns.

The experience gained at Kiradu seems to have encouraged the builder to experiment with even more slender and elegant columns in the two Navalakha temples at Sejakpur (Fig. 156) and Ghumli, in modern Kathiawar state. The basic form of the shikhara and the overall plan in its diagonal configuration remains the same. However, lifted up as the temples are on a beautiful horizontally delineated cushion like plinth (Fig. 156) they acquire a grace all their own. This quality is further enhanced by the columns, some of which are circular in profile. With their pronounced horizontal bands of delicate tracery like sculpture, they seem, as if turned out from an "embroidery stone lathe."

## THE SAS-BAHU IN GWALIOR

The architectural potential of the "Mandapa" of the Gujarat style can today be seen fully realised in a pair of temples, standing cheek by jowl within the fort of Gwalior in Madhya Pradesh. These too, like the Teli-ka-Mandir nearby (described earlier) are today popularly known by the curious name of Sas-bahu (literally mother-in-law—daughter-in-law) temples (Fig. 154). In the context of general Hindu structural timidity, only the Gujarat craftsman, with his skill in erecting columnar halls, could have conceived and built such daring structures. The volume of the Gujarat mandapa in either of the two temples explodes into a three tiered structure consisting of a maze of open galleries, and loggias, built around a central

154. Plan of the temple of Sas Bahu at Gwalior.

155. The larger Sas Bahu temple within the fort at Gwalior.

156. A view of the front portico of the Navlakha temple at Sejakhpur.

octagonal hall of over eighty feet height (Fig. 157). To support the massive receding masonry of the pyramidical roof the hall had to be provided with four central columns in addition to those of the octagonal ring. Though the dramatic quality of the interior space is somewhat diluted by the intrusion of these columns, it still makes a powerful impact. One cannot be certain whether the garbhagriha and shikhara attached to the mandapa were ever completed. Even if the builders had been able to erect one to match the proportions of the huge mandapa, no traces of the superstructure of either are extant.

The same fate has also overtaken a number of other temples in Gujarat where the shikharas have suffered great damage. Perhaps this could be reasonably attributed to the fact that a columnar construction for the mandapa akin to modern frame construction was, by its structural nature, better equipped to withstand the tremors of the great 9th century earthquake, than the solidly walled enclosures of garbhagriha (Fig. 155).

## MARBLE GLORIES OF DILWARA

It would seem that in Gujarat and Rajasthan the "tax set apart for the Jain gods" was greater than that set apart for the Hindu gods. This is not surprising. The affluence of the Jaina community was based entirely on commercial trade. Their rigid religious tenets of non-violence prevented a follower of the religion even from being an agriculturist, leave aside a warrior, since in ploughing the fields he was sure to kill many a live insects. The Jainas then had perforce gradually cornered commerce and trading as their main occupation. Ultimately, banking, trading and the power that went with it, was almost entirely controlled by the Jains. Therefore, when the Jains decided to build their temples at Dilwara near the modern hill resort of Mount Abu in Rajasthan, the expense involved in construction was of little consequence. While the Hindus had been content to build with the local golden brown sandstone, the Jains were not to be satisfied with anything so modest. They chose the finest; pure white marble was to be their chief building material. The fact that it had to be hoisted from the valley three thousand feet below at considerable cost and labour, was no deterrent to the prosperous Jainas.

## THE TEMPLE OF VIMALA SHAH

The famous temple founded by Vimala, typical of the many more that were built and are now in ruins, is set inside a

157. The mandapa of the Sas Bahu is an octagonal hall over 26 metre high that was the glory of the Hindu builder's structural capabilities.

rectangular courtyard (Fig. 161). The enclosing cells are a series of niches adorned with images of Tirathankars, or the "exalted ones" of the Jain religion. On the exterior the temple does not pretend to any architectural effects. In its plan too it is not dramatically different from the many Hindu temples of Gujarat. After passing through a domed entrance canopy and a hall filled with statuary portraying the Vimala family one approaches the main body of the temple that consists of the familiar octagonally planned mandapa connected to the shrine at the other end by a transept having two parallel rows of pillars. The temple strives to achieve its most dramatic response from the sheer profusion of carving over the entire body inside and out. The most exquisite feature in this sumptuous feast of sculpture is the ceiling over the central octagonal ring of the Mandapa (Fig. 159). The modestly proportioned dome constructed as ever by circular rings of oversailing masonry consists of eleven concentric friezes depicting patterns of figures and animals in procession. The lowest contains the forefronts and intertwined trunks of as many as 150 elephants. The dome culminates delicately in a pendant, suspended from the apex which carved out of pristine white almost translucent marble, looks like a fragile natural stalactite than a mere carving. Any real sense of architecture in the

159, 160, 161. The exquisite ceiling and mandapa of the Dilwara wherein a hard and adamant stone like marble is made to reproduce the fragility of snow flakes.

Vimala though is lost beneath the intricacy of carving and the profusion of detail (Fig. 160). So much so that even the natural delicate texture of marble is obscured having been fussed and fretted into excessive ornamentation. In spite of the fact that the ceiling of the dome really is like a "dream vision looming in the half-light" and the "figures have the fragility of snow-flakes," the perfection is of a rather mechanical character dependent as it is on the idea of creating impact through un-ceasing though perfect repetition. The overall impact of this shrine leaves one as cold as the marble of which it is created. Judging from the stern and forbidding visage of the God Mahavira (Fig. 161) installed in the cella, the designer had probably achieved the effect desired by the ascetic founder of the creed. However, at the same time there is no gainsaying the fact that "in its own ornate way the temple can be counted as among the architectural wonders (or rather curiosities) of the world."

## PICTURESQUE JAINA CITIES

As may be judged from the description of the above temple, the Jaina religion which had developed into a sort of theological mean between Hinduism and Buddhism, never quite acquired a distinct architectural style of its own. Rather the Jaina designer would borrow the shikhara motif when it so suited his fancy, and with equal casualness, he would plant a mini-Buddhist stupa right next to it. Also the mere ancientness of a temple, excepting of course obviously priceless edifices like that of the Vimala, did not add extra sacred value to the structure. In fact, the Jaina community seems to have frequently pulled down their old decaying buildings, to replace them by newer ones thereby leaving behind few examples of their earlier style. And so, what is largely left to us today of the Jaina tradition, is some very large and picturesque temple cities on the remote hills of Shatarunjya and Palitana in Kathiawar state (Fig. 162). Most of the temples of these cities are of recent origin, and are an unsynthesised agglomeration of many styles of building including even the Islamic. It may therefore be pertinent to reflect a while on the theories of the Hindu builders, that unlike the Jainas, exercised sufficient control over the millions of temples built all over the subcontinent to impart to its vast array of architecture a distinct and discernible style.

162. A view of the Jaina temple city on the Shatrunjaya hill at Palitana in Kathiawar state.

# 17

# The Mystique of the Vastupurusha-mandala

## The theories of Hindu architecture

DURING the medieval ages in India there was no single dynastic power that could be considered the undisputed dispenser of cultural and artistic ideas. Yet as we have seen Indian temple design, other than what may at best be described as regional flourishes, displayed a remarkable unity of aesthetic purposes. True the profile of the Shikhara varied from region to region, temples were at some places raised on monumental plinths and at other hidden behind cloisters; the number of mandapas preceding the deul or garbhagriha would be anything between one to four; these would either be placed along a single linear axis, or in concentric rings; a northern temple would have a shikhara and southern a Viamana. Nevertheless, the evolution of each of these seemingly disparate elements was always motivated by a unified philosophy of design that permeated into the remotest corners where the Hindu craftsmen were at work.

## THE TRABEATE SYSTEM

One obvious example of the Hindus' self defined parameters is the universal adoption of the trabeate system of construction. It is strange that the structural economics of using the arch vault or other mechanical means, which from the early Roman times were commonly employed all over the world never became popular in India. The Indian builder, through centuries of development, was quite content to use the often wasteful system of vertical columns and horizontal lintels, of stone or timber, supported by brackets if necessary, to cover his roof or span openings. A facile though poetic excuse for eschewing the use of the arch proferred by the Hindu builder was that "the arch never sleeps." As a rational result, however, the use of mortar was dispensed with, there being virtually no inclined pressures to distribute between the courses of masonry.

## THE BRAHMINS MAKE THE RULES

This persistent uniformity of content and techniques is reminiscent too of the rather mechanical standardisation of the ancient Indus Valley civilisation. It could have been the result only of some kind of absolute and unbreakable rules governing the building craft. Not those laid down by a political power since from the Gupta period up to the 14th century, when Moghul rule was established, there was no single political power of any consequence. A unified authority, if any, was wielded only by the priestly Brahmin class. They had, as we have seen, cleverly inviegled themselves into a position of controlling every facet of Hindu activity—bureaucratic, commercial, domestic and, of course, religious. No ceremonial activity be it a birth, a death, marriage, reaching puberty, building a house or starting a commercial enterprise could take place without the consent of the learned Brahmins. This was generally granted after payment for the performance of elaborate rituals, due commissions in cash or gold and also if the nature of the venture permitted a continuing share of the profits. The art of building was not going to be an exception to the Brahmins merciless iron web.

## COSMOLOGY AND ARCHITECTURE

The basic concepts of temple design were evolved through the creative activity of master craftsmen. It was nevertheless the Brahmins, who began laying down elaborate and complex rules of layouts for building. These were intentionally made complex enough to be well beyond the comprehension of a layman or even a skilled craftsman and consequently beyond his rights to challenge. In the great Hindu compendiums of architectural rules "the Vastushastra" there is much that is deliberate esoteric mumbo-jumbo. The very minutest of the acts of building, such as the layout, choice of site, testing of soil conditions and even the thickness of walls and columns were based not on technological, but rather on mythological and even astronomical consideration. This is often carried to a ludicrous extent. Formulae are drawn up to indicate how the thickness of a wall, or the span between the columns of a temple was to be determined from the day or time when construction commenced; the orientation of the temple; the caste of the major donor and even the position of the stars in the sky. Needless to say, under such circumstances, creativity of the building craftsmen had to be carried out within the theological disciplines framed by the priests in the "Vastushastras."

The myriads of temples all over India are an eloquent testimony to the indefatigable Indian craftsman, who was able to create such beautiful works of art, in spite of the countless restrictions placed on him. For this he must thank the integrity of the traditions of his craft which being more ancient than that of the Brahmins, proved to be equally durable and tenacious. To him this sacred heritage was enshrined in the so called "Senis" or ancient guilds of craftsmen.

## "SENIS"—THE INDIAN CRAFT GUILDS

Even during the formative stages of the art in India, building craftsmen recognised not only the specialised quality of their skill, but also of its intrinsic value to society. As early as the seventh century B.C. when building activity was carried out with temporary materials like timber and unbaked brick, craftsmen had organised themselves into guilds to effectively guard their economic, technical and artistic interests. An association of this nature, in its earlier stages would accept "antevasikas" (literally the boarders), as resident apprentices, to train them in the skills of their crafts. Over a period of time when the more laborious arts of cave and stone architecture became popular, the trainee required not only long periods of theoretical instruction, but also practical experience at sites often remote from urban centres.

Under such circumstances, heredity became a custom. The skills of the trade were conveniently passed on from father to son. At the earliest opportunity the son was given a chisel and hammer and trained to give shape to a block of rough quarried stone, carving of finer details being left to the father. Often during the construction of a single enormous venture, the son would acquire the skill of his father, to take his own rightful place as a master craftsman. The builder though working for the property owning wealthy class, himself rarely acquired any immovable property that he could leave to his sons. The convention of heredity, apart from its practical function, assured the skilled artisan that his son would atleast continue to retain his status in society. The transfer of skills to his offspring was the craftsman's insurance policy on his skills.

## SCHOOLS OF STYLE

On some occasions the magnitude of their task would force "a group of craftsmen to settle down near the site of their labours for a generation or more." It was such a settlement at a single site, rather than purely academic thought, that resulted in the growth of an Art Centre, giving rise to a school and a style of architecture. So it was, that a group of craftsmen working continuously for over a century on the building ventures of the Chandelas, gradually evolved the characteristic Khajuraho style. Or those concentrated around Bhubaneswar formulated the Orissan mode of building.

In spite of their rigorous and obscure rules, the Indian cannons, or rather "ordinances of art" (which had to be memorised by one ambitious enough to become a master craftsman) had their own positive value. Architect Le Corbusier claims that his theory of proportions "the Module, made the bad impossible and the good easy," has rarely been put to test. The practising contemporary architect never quite took to it as his design gospel. Percy Brown's assessment of the Indian counterpart 'The Mandala,' that "if faithfully followed, would make failure impossible," is however, not an empty claim. It is a fact, borne out by the quality of Indian temple activity through centuries and spread over territories separated by thousands of miles.

## THE MAGIC OF THE SQUARE

Confronted with the myriads of exotic forms of the Hindu temple, it is difficult to believe that the crux of the guiding philosophy of design of the Mandala was the square; most basic, rational and elementary of all geometric forms. For the earthly abode of God there could be nothing but the most perfect of forms obviously either the circle (a polygon of infinite sides) or a square (a polygon of equal sides joined at right angles). The Hindu chose the square. The circle, which had been adopted by the Buddhists for reasons of their own, to the Hindu represented movement, as inherent in a wheel, or in the ever-mobile spherical forms of the universal cosmos.

163. The square Mandala or Divine Chart of the Hindu builder.

164. The various deities around Brahma in the Mandala.

165. The Hindu Vastupurshamandala consists of a human figure in a Yogic posture, enclosed within a square.

The Hindu's aim was quite contrary. His temples were meant to be permanent abode for his otherwise heavenly and elusive gods. Their images had to be installed in shapes symbolising stability rather than mobility. The square fulfilled his aims far more appropriately.

The square Mandala (at best "divine chart" in English) was divided into so many equal squares—that containing 64 or 81 (Fig. 163) being the most popular. The priest then invested each of the squares with metaphysical and magic powers, by locating an individual deity in each. The position of each subdivided square in the total represented the power or otherwise the deity attributed to it. Thus, Brahma, the Supreme God, creator, preserver and destroyer, invariably occupied the central square or group of squares. Lesser deities were posted in the four corners (the germ of the Panchratna plan) and more minor one filled up the balance (Fig. 164). To invest the square with a human quality, apart from its divine one, it was shown as being able to accommodate within itself a human figure, though in a contorted Yogic pose (Fig. 165).

175

## HUMANISM IN THE SQUARE

In investing the dimensions of architecture with this human quality, the Hindu mind had preceded Leonardo da Vinci, who hundreds of years later demonstrated how a circle could be drawn to contain a human figure with outstretched hands and feet (Fig. 166) or even Corbusier's theory of "the Modular" that was built around human dimensions (Fig. 167). The Hindu priest's humane touch to architecture was however quite different. In his case it is clear that it is not that the square was really inspired by the human body, rather the form of the Purusha (human) was made to suit the abstract idea of the square as the geometric form supreme.

166. The renaissance concept of the human figure in a circle.

167. Corbusier's modular and the human scale.

Having acquired magical, geomantic as well as human properties, the emerging chart called the "Vastupurushmandala" (literally the magic chart of the architecture of the Supreme man), was now fit to be transformed into an architectural ground plan for a temple. In its simplest form the outer ring of squares could denote the thickness of the walls of the garbhagriha (Fig. 168). On another scale four central squares could constitute the inner cell surrounded by a ring of 12 squares which became the walls and the next 16 or 28 the pradakshina-path and outer wall and so on (Fig. 169).

The elementary division was only the first step towards the building up of a rather complex system. With a bit of artistic license, the Mandala could be expanded to generate the most elaborate of forms, the basic unit of these always being the square (Fig. 170). And so the large square was sub-divided into thousands of small squares by the architect. This enabled him to add sculptural richness to his wall surfaces by the simple expedient of treating the Mandala virtually like a graph paper adding a unit here and setting one back there, not unlike the modern architect's structural grid. It was with an artistic manipulation of the grid ordained by the "Vastupurushamandala" that the Indian architect created the profusion of exotic shapes and forms that are the temples of India.

168, 169. The Hindu Vastupurshamandala transformed into architectural plans.

170. Plan of the Ambarnath temple, showing 1. Garbhagriha and 2. Mandapa.

But again, though the very form of the shikhara defied measurement through right angles and sqaures, the theoretician left little allowance for blunders in its profile. He ensured that the curve of this essentially bamboo shape was translated accurately into stone, by meticulously plotting it out against the curves of more precise geometric forms like the ellipse (Fig. 171). Furthermore, the entire structure was classified into many smaller elements, each with its own defined function, and with names, analogous to parts of the human body.

## "ALIVE" AND "DEAD" MATERIALS

To make such abstract laws of geometry work in building practise, the Hindu cannons propounded a truly unique theory of building materials and their structural properties. Materials were classified either as "alive" or "dead". The wood in a growing tree was "alive," and its structural properties were therefore to be respected. Once felled, the timber obtained from it however was "dead". It became a material to be used and shaped according to the purely artistic inclinations and whims of the architect and the technical capacity of the craftsman. No wonder then that the more ductile form of rock cut architecture proved to be the true metier for the expression of the Indian architectural genius. On the other hand, in dealing with structural buildings, the Hindu architect never worried much about exploiting the "true" structural potential of a material but was more concerned with using it to fulfil his aesthetic intentions.

We have evidence of this in massive sculptural works in stone like the Kailasa, which were covered with a uniform layer of plaster to look like the Himalayas; or walls of baked bricks which were cut and embossed as blocks of stone normally would be as in the brick temple at Bhitargaon. Earlier stone masons had cut and shaped blocks of stone into needles and posts as they would be sawn out of timber. These were even assembled together into the famous Buddhist railings, with a moritce and tenon joint, more logical to carpentry than stone masonry. The patient Hindu craftsman, intent on giving permanent form to his visions, was not unduly bothered by such technical naiceties. Rather he created a peculiar kind of drama by forcing the will of his abstract artistic theories on materials not readily suited for them.

171. The mathematics of the parabolic shikhara.

# 18

# The Splendours of medieval India

## The "cathedrals" of Modhera, Konarak and Khajuraho

WE have examined in the last chapter the recondite theories and formulae of architecture laid down in the Hindu manuals. The Indian craftsman had experienced centuries of familiarity and practise with them. Now from the 10th century onwards, he was taking up the challenge of erecting great temple cathedrals in different parts of north India. Three of the more significant achievements in the west, central and eastern regions of India, range from Modhera in Gujarat to Khajuraho in Madhya Pradesh and Konarak in Orissa. Being representative of the architectural qualities inspired by the regional styles they are worthy of comparison, as being the finest achievements of three great schools of Gujarat, Khajuraho and Orissa.

### THE SUN TEMPLE, MODHERA

The acme of the Gujarat craftsman's art was the temple of the Sun God of Modhera (Fig. 173) erected in 1026, on a site 18 miles south-east of modern Patan. Temples to the Sun God, even in distant parts of India, have had a curiously uniform pattern of development and decay. The temples of Martand, Konarak, Orissa, and Suraj Kund in Delhi, all seem to have been constructed on specially selected sites away from the humdrum of daily urban life; they are unusually ambitious efforts and each one has lain deserted and ignored by the devout pilgrims for the past many centuries. Nevertheless, even in their derelict splendour, they bear testimony, if nothing else, to the ambitions of both the builder and his feudal lords (Fig. 172).

Built most probably under the patronage of the Solankis, the Sun Temple of Modhera too is no exception to the ravages of time. "What, at one time, may have been a site endowed with considerable sacred sanctity, is today a village of mud huts," close to the ruins of a once grand Sun Temple. The various constituents of this temple, the huge bathing tank, columnar Sabha Mandapa, a peristyler assembly hall and shrine, are knit together into an "entirely organic plan in the relation of all the parts of the shrine to the whole, and its functional arrangements of all the architectural accessories of religious worship."

The huge rectangular tank for ritualistic ablutions, lies beneath the main eastern approach to the temple. Water was contained within buttressed walls that are a maze of steps and terraces, interspersed with mini shrines—an architectural and engineering masterpiece in its own right. A broad flight of

172. A view of the existing mandapa of the Sun temple at Modhera, as seen from the bathing tank.

173. Plan of the Sun temple at Modhera in Gujarat, showing 1. Prasada, 2. Gudha mandapa and 3. Sabha mandapa

174, 175. The sabha mandapa and the sensuous pillars of Modhera.

steps takes one up to what was a torana archway resting on two gracefully moulded columns. The profile of the capital shaft and base of each of these is all contained within one sweeping rythmic curve (Fig. 174) typical of the gracefully sensuous style of Modhera. Immediately behind the torana lies the sabha-mandapa, planned (Fig. 175) in the usual Gujarat style around an octagonal pillared space. Sloping seats and dwarf columns are set in rectangular offsets around its periphery. As in the other temples of Gujarat, it is this mandapa that is both the functional and visually vibrant heart of the whole complex. The shafts of each of its columns are exquisitely almost embroidered with scrolls of ornamentation interspersed with sculptures of gods and goddesses. The pillars on the periphery of the central octagonal space are laced together by delicately carved interlinked sinuous brackets aptly referred to as "flying toranas." The rest of the temple comprising the garbhagriha and attached mandapa has virtually vanished. It was a conventional walled structure its ornamentation though was in perfect consonance with gracefully echoing the rythmic lines of the main mandapa. This entire edifice, raised as it was over a massive rectangular stylobate must have been a fitting tribute to the great god that it purported to worship and honour. "To see even the ruins of this noble monument not only rising like an exaltation but mirrored in the still waters below, is to feel that the creator was more than a great artist, but a weaver of dreams."

## THE SUN TEMPLE, KONARAK

In paying their homage to the same god, the dreams of the master craftsman of Orissa, were of a different nature altogether. They decided to house their Sun god literally as Indian mythology has conceived it; "blazing his way through the heavens on the chariot of time pulled by seven leaping and prancing magnificient horses." This remote site was located on the sea coast of Orissa, away from the traditional and thriving religious centres of Bhubaneshwar and Puri.

To simulate the appearance of a ratha, or wheeled car, the longer sides of the terrace over which the temple was erected were ornamented with reliefs of twelve meticulously carved massive wheels, more than 10 feet (3 metres) in diameter. Each of these giant wheels is a faithful reproduction in stone of its original, complete with a hub, timber pins and spokes, all profusely and meticulously sculptured (Fig. 178). The parapets on either sides of the flight of steps rising up to the entrance are in fact a row of life size sculptures of "richly caprisoned steeds, rearing and staining in their harness, as they strive to drag the great bulk (of the temple) along." Over the main platform are placed the combination of Jagmohan and Deul. On another high plinth facing the majestic flight of steps leading to the shrine is situated the Nat Mandir which is a modest sized replica of the Jagmohan. The entire complex (Fig. 176) including also a subsidiary shrine to Ramachandra and a refactory of utilitarian design is set within a vast enclosure of 865 feet (263.6 metres) by 540 feet (164.5 metres). Presumably, the enclosing wall, the superstructure of which has altogether vanished, was provided with three pyramidical roofed gateways located in the centres of its eastern, northern and southern walls.

176. A conjectural restoration of the grand complex of Konarak as it must have been in its full glory in 1250 A.D.

**177.** One of the gigantic larger than life, full bodied sculptures on the eaves of the Jagmohan of the Sun temple at Konarak and a view of the existing ruins of Konarak.

## FAILURE OF STRUCTURE

The shikhara over the deul containing an image of the sun god carved in chlorite was envisaged to ascend to a height of over 200 feet (60.8 metres). The substantial masonry necessary for such a grand shikhara, was wide enough to enclose three subsidiary shrines, each approached by an individual external staircase. Even so, the ambitions of its chief patron, King Narshimdeva (1238-64) were well beyond the technical skill of his craftsmen. The massive shikhara is today only a "battered and broken pile of masonry." The tower most likely never rose to its intended height, since the foundations started sinking before its completion. The 100 feet (30 metres) high cubic mass of the Jagmohan built over massive and thick stone walls was given additional support in the form of four massive central piers, spanned by stone lintels reinforced even with wrought iron beams. In spite of these precautions sometime in the 19th century the interior of the hall was made inaccessible as it had to be completely blocked with rubble from inside to prevent its corbelled roof from caving in.

## TRIUMPH OF SCULPTURE

Even from the ruins of the great Sun Temple, it is obvious that the massive proportions of the temple were no deterrent to the sculptor. In addition to the traditional massive reliefs that cover the entire outer surface, he also proceeded to adorn the gigantic pyramidical roof of the Jagmohan. As a result of its massive size, the diminishing tiers of its roof are interspread with what become broad platforms rather than mere steps. Inspired by the overpowering scale of the architectural backdrop the Indian sculptor planted full bodied statues of heroic dimensions along the edges of the lowest platform (Fig. 177). Each of these represents a musician gracefully contributing his mite to a silent but mighty orchestra in stone. In spite of the fact that this was the Hindu sculptors first attempt at embellishing an architectural facade with completely free standing statuary he executed the job with his usual consummate mastery. It is clear then, that the remains of the grand temple complex as they stand today are more a tribute to the Indian carftsman's sculptural skills than his structural ingenuity.

178. The Stone wheels of the Sun God's chariot each of which is more than 3 metre in diameter and profusely sculptured.

179. Plan of the great 10th century Kandarya Mahadeo temple, Khajuraho, showing 1. Garbhagriha, 2. Antrayla, 3. Mandapa and 4. Ardha mandapa.

## THE KANDARYA MAHADEV, KHAJURAHO

In contrast, the builders of Khajuraho, both artistically and structurally, were more successful in erecting their piece-de-resistance; the temple cathedral of Kandarya Mahedev. In expanding the plan of the temple to contain four, instead of the more usual two compartments, the designer never lost sight of the necessary inter-relationship of each to the whole (Fig. 179). The result—a perfectly balanced and composed elevation, its components like so many masses, gracefully inter-linked with each other (Fig. 180). All the elements of a full bodied temple containing the garbhagriha, a sourrounding pradakshina-path, antaralaya, mandapa and ardha-mandapa, become the cells of a unfied organism. The first four are compactly enclosed within a continuous peripheral wall pierced only by beautifully crafted balconies. Just enough light is admitted through these to bring the profusely sculptured surfaces of the

180. Elevation of the Kandarya Mahadeo, Khajuraho.

interior to life (Fig. 181). The roof of the ardha-mandapa on the other hand is held up on columns, and is an appropriately extended version of the entrance portico.

It is true that the height of the temple spire (116 feet) (35 metres) is little more than half that envisaged for the Great Sun Temple at Konarak. But the quadruplicated application of the "Urusringas" described earlier, and the soaring vertical lines of the shikhara, accelerate the vision along the crescendo of curves, reaching out to the heavenly gods, as it were. These all create an illusion of height, that Konarak even if completed may well never have achieved. The vertical volumes of the shikharas of Khajuraho take off from an adequately cushioned base of marked horizontality, which is preserved right up to the level of the balconies in the outer walls. The dark voids of interspersed balconies and the open pillared mandapa in front create the impression of a massive pile of masonry, poised delicately over slender columns, adding a subtle touch of lightness to the virtual mountains of stone (Fig. 182).

181. Architectonics of the interior of the Kandarya Mahadeo come to life under the light filtering in through the side balconies.

182. A massive pile of masonry delicately poised over slender columns; the temple of Kandarya Mahadeo.

# THE EROTICA OF HINDU TEMPLES

Apart from all their points of difference, a feature that is common both to Konarak and Khajuraho, is the remarkable profusion of the now famous erotic sculpture on the temple walls. To a certain degree, erotic or at least highly suggestive sculpture and painting, are common in Indian temples, almost from the earliest times. They can be passed off as expressions of the Indian craftsman's "love for life in all its aspects." But the erotica of Khajuraho and Konarak is another thing altogether. The elaborate and extremely graphic presentation here is not restricted merely to amorous embraces or copulation between man and woman, but includes also, what progressive terminology would describe as free group sex, and the conservative as downright perverse and degenerate orgies.

The fantastic variety and exuberance of such erotica has prompted comments covering a wide spectrum of thought. To the devout defenders of the moral purity of Hindu faith "this evil erotica, is purposefully perpetrated ugliness to ward off the evil eye" or "a device to highlight the contrast between the evil outside and the purity of the inner sanctum"; the latter supported by the fact that erotic sculpture is to be found only on the outer walls and never inside. Some believe that the erotica was inspired by various tribal tantric rights, which along with their unlimited sexual license, had been absorbed into Hindu mythology. To the more outspoken, however, it was nothing more than the downright immorality that had crept into the courtly life of the kings, and the religious life of the priests. This section of opinion derives peculiar satisfaction from the conjecture that the once powerful Chandelas vanished from the scene so quickly after building such great temples, only because of their excessive indulgence in such immoral acts.

## A FREUDIAN CATHARSIS

On the other end of the scale are the Freudian thinkers. The theme of sex and other libidinous excesses that are so vividly depicted here to them is the manifestation of a whole society undergoing a monumental catharsis, to purify itself of all its sins. A few would probably agree that pure erotica was only a logical conclusion to the theme of "love for all aspects of life," sex being an undeniably important "aspect" of life. Redundant to add that the Brahmin keeper of the temple was reluctant to be left out of any "aspect" of life, particularly of

183. Left and above, erotica at the Sun temple, Konarak and on the base of the Kandarya Mahadeo temple at Khajuraho.

course of one as immortal as sex. So why should not the walls of his temple become inviting visual lessons in the irrepressible art of sexual enjoyment. The cynics have even unabashedly suggested that the Brahmin having earnt his due from performing the marriage ceremony posted erotica on his temples to ensure continued indulgence by the novice couple, in affairs of the temple. That the Brahmin judged human nature with astute shrewdness, is more than amply proven by the worldwide undying fame of the erotica of Khajuraho.

Whatever the causes, there is little doubt that in the display of excessive erotica, the Indian sculptor carried out his master's bidding, with if anything an even greater skill and sense of plastic beauty (Fig. 183) than he lavished on statues of the gods themselves.

# 19

# Cholas and Pandyas, the magnificient Tamils

## Tanjore and soaring Gopurams

IN the south too, like in the north, the 10th and 11th centuries constituted the age of "Temple Cathedrals." As the great Chola dynasty began to dominate the southern country the refined "Little gems" of the Pallava period were no longer an adequate expression of its majestic power. The Cholas desired something grander in conception to immortalise their glory. The craftsmen having acquired long experience in the skills of stone masonry, were more than qualified to carry out their masters' grandiose schemes.

### GREAT TEMPLE, TANJORE

Once Thanjavur (modern Tanjore) fell to the Chola king Rajaraja the Great (985-1081), he commissioned the Brihedesvara temple (Fig.184), the size alone of which was a gigantic step forward in the evolution of religious architecture in the south. Until now, even after 500 years of building experience, no tower higher than 60 feet (18.2 metres) had been attempted by the Hindu craftsmen of India. But the masons of Tanjore now set out to make amends for the timidity of the southern builders in one big leap by conceiving of a spire, more than three times the maximum height achieved so far. An ambitious superstructure required that the cellas be proportionately enlarged in plan (Fig.185). In the great temple of Tanjore, it became a massive square of 82 feet (24.9 metres) side, containing within it a pradakshina path, running all the way around the cella. The cube of the garbhagriha was carried vertically up to a height of 50 feet (15 metres). Thereafter the familiar pyramidical tower soared another 130 feet (39.6 metres) into the sky, capped by a single enormous domical stone weighing more than 80 tons.

Two flat roofed mandapas in front of the Vimana are placed as always along the central axis, largeness of their size in keeping with the proportions of the Vimana. The portico housing the sculpture of the Holy Nandi bull is situated along the same axis but is detached from the main temple, much like the sabha-mandapa of the Sun Temple at Modhera and the Nat Mandir of Konarak. The entire complex stands today in the middle of a quadrangle defined by a peripheral verandah of two rows of columns.

The 200 feet (60.8 metres) high stone tower (Fig.186) which rises impressively over the sea of courtyards around, is a gigantic reproduction of the familiar Dravidian Vimana. However, the horizontal tiers of its thirteen storeys have been suppressed to accentuate the soaring verticality of the conver-

**184.** The over 55 metre high vimana of the 10th century Brihideswara at Tanjore capped by a single piece domical stone weighing over 80 tonnes.

194

185. Plan of the great Brihidesvara temple, Tanjore.
1. Garbhagriha, 2. Pradakshina, 3. Mahamandapa and 4. Nandi

186. The vimana of the great temple Tanjore over the courtyards around.

ging lines of the truncated pyramid. This Vimana, though only a few feet less in height than the projected height of the shikhara of Konarak, and almost as old, has withstood the ravages of over 900 years, literally without a dent. In constructing it the south Indian craftsman showed a greater understanding of structural principles. It may be argued that in choosing the simpler and more stable form of the pyramid he was on safer grounds than the northern builder struggling with the more complex curvilinear shape of the shikhara. But this would not be entirely true; as we shall see, he soon proved himself equally adept at constructing structures of equally complicated nature, endowed with enduring stability.

## EXPANSIONISM OF THE CHOLAS

Rajaraja the great was followed by his son Rajendra I, who continued the expansionist policies of his father. His ambitions, however, were not restricted merely to subduing the neighbouring Chalukyas who were in control of the trading ports of modern Malabar. He moved much further afield and sent a Chola expedition north east across Orissa which is said to have reached the holy waters of the distant river Ganga. The Cholas were also engaged in trading activities with China and to safeguard their shipping interests, they waged a successful campaign against the Kingdom of Shrivijaya (the Southern Malay Peninsula and Sumatra). Closer at home, the threat posed by the triangular alliance of Kerala, Srilanka and the Pandyas, was also crushed by Chola pressure. The Cholas eventually over-ran and devasted Anurandhpura the Capital city of Srilanka, and set up a new capital at Pollaonnurva.

# THE TEMPLE OF GANGAIKONDACHOLAPURAM

Growing Chola power was accompanied by an equally passionate desire to build new cities, that would be an appropriate architectural symbol of their expanding empire. Kingly ambitions were reflected in Rajendra 1's decision to challenge the glory of Thanjavur by shifting his seat of power to Gangaikondacholapurm (28 kilometres from modern Kumbhakonam). The spirit of the times dictated that the most dominant edifice of the new city be a monumental temple. The greatness of an Indian city of the middles ages was measured not by its town planning wonders, nor its streets and bazaars and houses, but rather by the magnificence of the temple housing the presiding deity. Today though, all that the deity of Gangaikondacholapuram "presides over" is a few straggling village huts, Rajendra's great city having long ago crumbled into dust. The city temple though reduced to ruins, is a flamboyant reminder of vanished Chola glory.

187. The fluid lines of the vimana of the Great Chola temple at Gangaikondacholapuram (1025 A.D.).

188. Plan (above) and section (below) of the Gangaikondacholapuram temple. 1 Garbhagriha, 2. Mahamandapa; 3. Mandapa and 4. Nandi.

Though architects of King Rajendra have obviously modelled their temple in essence of design as well as scale, on the great temple of Tanjore, they made some refreshing innovations nevertheless. The main Vimana (Fig. 187) rising from a base even larger than that at Tanjore, is transformed into a form embodying concave quoins, at the ends of convex planes of sculptured surfaces. In contrast to "the rigid and geometrically perfect Vimana of Tanjore, that symbolises conscious might, the fluid lines of the latter are imbued with a subconscious grace." The Mandapa of this temple on the other hand is totally different from the concept of Thanjavur. It is a huge flat-roofed hall of 75′ × 195′ (22.8 × 59.4 metres). The entire structure is built on a high platform. The approach aisles, designed like processional paths, however are left at ground level. With the Hindu builder's aversion to any system of construction other than the trabeate, it was inevitable that such a large room be held up by a veritable forest of over 150, closely spaced, slender columns (Fig. 188). The first of its kind, this hall foreshadows the emergence of the famous "halls of thousand columns" of later temple complexes.

## THE TRIUMPH OF THE PANDYAS

With the death of Rajendra I in about 1050 A.D. his successors continued to maintain communications with the Chinese, to sustain their commerce. King Kulothunga even sent an embassy of seventy-two merchants to negotiate trade agreements with China. Nearer home, their peninsular neighbours however were forces to contend with. Even though the Cholas' sacked the Chalukyan Capital of Kalyani, they were unable to decimate the seemingly indefatigable Chalukyans. Rather, the rivalry between the two was only further intensified. The southern triumvirate of the Pandyas, Keralas and Srilanka too never gave the later Cholas, sufficiently long periods of respite to indulge in building ventures on the Tanjore scale. Gradually sapped of their strength after 800 years of indisputable sway over the Tamil country, the Cholas ultimately succumbed to the Pandyas in the middle of the 14th century.

The Pandyas inherited both the wealth of the trade that the Cholas had established with the Chinese and the splendour of their trading cities. The kings continued to live in great luxury and magnificence. Marco Polo passing through India on his return from China, described the port town of Kayal (today marked by a few fishermen's huts on the beach) as a "great and noble city" and the king as one who "wore upon his person the most costly jewels." By the times of the Pandyas however, dramatic changes had taken place in the polity of the north. A rather incomprehensible force had crossed over through the Khyber Pass and established domination in the northern regions. This was the armies of the followers of a new and unvanquished religion—that of Islam. They had by now established their Capital city at Delhi and were beginning to make inroads into the Hindu empires of the Deccan.

## THE SANCTITY OF THE ANCIENT

As during the later Chola period, construction activity, as far as new massive undertakings were concerned, continued to languish during Pandyan suzeranity, though for different reasons. While the temples of Tanjore and Gangakonda-Cholapuram, adequately glorified the power of the Hindu gods as well as the Chola kings, they never became popular centres of worship. The religious sentiment of the people was directed more towards ancient temples in spite of the fact that these were modest in size and possessed of little architectural significance. To the devotee, however, old was gold, and to him these historic shrines were endowed with "marked sanctity because enshrined within them were images of deep and lasting veneration." To replace or materially change the outer shell of these ancient consecrated images merely to enlarge them in size, would have been a sacrilegious act. And so a good deal of the energies of the building craftsmen under the Pandyas was concentrated in the maintenance, addition of ancillaries and the enlargement and protection of such ancient structures.

## BATTLEMENTS OF PROTECTION

To guard their immense wealth, high walls of a purely utilitarian character, often battlemented and provided with platforms were hurriedly built around a number of such sacred temples. Such activity was no doubt, prompted also by the imminent danger of Muslim invasion from the north. The infamous sack of Somnath and the daring raids of Allaudin right up to Deogiri were dreaded and fresh memories. The external appearance of many an ancient shrine was thus forcibly reduced to the plainness of a fortress—a function that the temple could actually be called upon to fulfil in an emergency.

## GATEWAYS TO TEMPLES

This state of affairs however could not be allowed to last for long. The problem facing the royal patrons was of adding architectural status to the insignificant ancient shrines lost within its protective battlements. Finally, the Pandyan designers hit upon the idea of erecting lofty gateways at the entrance points in the walls. This served the two-fold object of alleviating the monotonous drabness of the enclosure, and at the same time endowing the temple precincts with appropriate visual impact. The Pandyan builders were now called in to erect these monumental passageways. During subsequent periods of peace and security, lofty portals or Gopurams. (Fig. 189) (literally the Cow-Gate, from rural Aryan terminology) could be erected in the outer walls, without disrupting the ritual or endangering the security of the temple.

## THE EVOLUTION OF THE GOPURAM

Inevitably, an entrance to the house of "God" had to be a massive form towering into the sky and visible for miles around.

189. Section of a typical southern Gopuram.

Yet it was undesirable to rival or repeat the architectonics of the Vimana of the inner cella, the holy of the holies. In any case, the square plan of the garbhagriha was hardly an appropriate one for a gateway; a square apart from its sacred sanctity, had a sense of firmness and finality about it. On the other hand, the ideal design of an entrance porticullis would be one that conveyed a sense of transition from outside towards the inner sanctum. A broad side on rectangular plan conveyed this intention more appropriately than the square (Fig. 190). Thus, the base of the gateway became a vertical pile of masonry rising over the oblong of the plan. The central opening was spanned by means of massive lintels of stone. If the size demanded, a system of projecting brackets was inserted on either side, to reduce the span of the lintels (Fig. 191).

Over this substantial base, built in stone, rose a pyramidal structure composed as ever of diminishing tiers generally built in brick and plaster. The topmost tier like the base from which it had emerged was also a rectangle in plan. It would thus not be appropriate to crown it with the familiar octagonal domical stone, which sat more comfortably over a square plan. Moreover, such a symbol associated as it was with the sacred tower over the central shrine, belonged to a higher religious hierarchy. Looking back to the wide array of the religious and secular forms of the past, for an adequate alternative, the craftsmen found that the barrel vault roof of the rectangular Buddhist chaitya hall served his purpose eminently. This functional form, reduced now to an ornamental solid shape, crowned with a row of finials over the ridge, proved a fitting climax for his soaring tower (Fig. 192). Every inch of the surface of the body of the Gopuram was covered of course, with the usual efflorescence of tiers upon tiers of sculptured and even polychromed gods, apsaras and demons. Over a period of time, a number of such towers rising around a temple became the familiar skyline of any sizable urban settlement in the southern country (Fig. 193). The temple had by now evolved into the centre not only of the religious but also social, economic and cultural life of the urbanites. The maintenance and financing of this social centre was comparable to that of any large scale institution of modern times. In its heyday, the Great Temple of Tanjore for example had an "annual income of 500 lb troy of precious stones and 600 lb troy of silver. It kept in reasonable comfort any army of 212 attendants, 57 musicians and 400 women entertainers apart from the many hundreds of priests."

190, 191, 192. The evolution of the form of the Gopuram, derived as it was from a rectangular prismatic base, and a pyramid crowned with a barrel vaulted form derived from the Buddhist Chaitya.

193. A number of Gopurams placed along the cardinal axis of a South Indian temple.

## SOCIOLOGY OF THE CITY TEMPLE

The temple also generated steady income by financing commercial enterprises and acting as bankers and money lenders. Another perpetual source of income was the socalled devadasis. Originally, they may well have been a venerated group of women attendants donated by wealthy parents at an early age to the temple, not unlike the vestal Virgins of Rome. Some of them were painstakingly trained by the learned priest in the art of south Indian classical dance, of Bharat Natyam. A larger number of them however were reduced to prostitutes operating under a religious umbrella enriching the coffers of the temples.

Such a phenomenal growth in the functions of the temple naturally demanded a corresponding physical growth. However, having enclosed their temple precincts within a forbidding wall, the only way to acquire more land for the complex was to throw another concentric ring of even larger battlements, punctuated by equally huge Gopurams. The seeds of the growth of a temple akin to the annual rings around the trunk of a tree was thus firmly sown. As we shall see the germ of this idea led to the evolution of the great "Temple cities" of Madurai and Rameswaram.

# 20

# The Hoysalas of the Karnataka

## "Star" temples in Halebid and Belur

IN the deeper south, as we have just seen, builders were kept occupied by what contemporary architectural parlance would describe as "addition and alteration jobs." In the northwestern reaches of the peninsula meanwhile an entirely new form of building activity was beginning. The Muslim rulers of the Delhi Sultanate, having established their power over most of the Gangetic plain, were now steadily pushing southwards. A good number of craftsmen, concerned less with religious loyalties and more with exploiting their professional and technical skill, were absorbed into the construction of edifices for the Muslim rulers. Temple building activity of any consequence was virtually at an end in the north and the more orthodox master craftsmen were immigrating southwards to seek the patronage of the surviving Hindu courts.

The northern Deccan region between the river Tapti and the river Kistna was controlled by the Yadavas who had thrown off the Chalukya yoke. They were not averse to employing these craftsmen to promote a building style distinct from that of their former overlords. The craftsmen, seeking refuge in the south were descendants of those who had evolved the Gujarat style under the once powerful Solanki dynasty. Architecturally speaking the Yadav country gradually became a provincial outpost of Gujarat. The 13th century temples of this region do show some signs of originality but in substance they are largely variations on the themes of Gujarat.

An example of this is the Ambernath Temple (Fig. 194) at modern Thana near Bombay. In plan, it follows the familiar arrangement of the mandapa and the cella placed in a diagonal relationship—a planning device that was popular under the Solankis. In the true Gujarat tradition, the craftsmen have really gone to town in decorating the walls and ceilings of the temples with finely crafted details. The wealth of sculptural figures and the series of projections and recesses are piled up with "ornament upon ornament producing a bewildering tumult of sculptured forms." The tumult continues even into the roof of the mandapa, which is a pyramidical pile of miniature reproductions of its own architectural form (Fig. 195). Though the Ambernath, like so many others in Gujarat has lost its shikhara, the temple at Sunnar in Nasik is better preserved. It is a temple of the Panchtayana class, standing in the middle of a wide platform with miniature shrines at each corner. The tower over the central shrine is a series of full bodied shikhara like.

195. The pile up of mini-shikharas in the Ambarnath temple.

194. The 11th century Ambarnath temple at Thana near Bombay; plan half looking up and half looking down, showing the elaborate geometry of floor and ceiling patterns.

## THE HOYSALAS AND NORTHERN INFLUENCE

Soon, however, with the ominous shadow of Muslim power spreading further the Hindu craftsman was pushed deeper south into the region around modern Mysore. Here a tribe of hill chieftains known as the Hoysalas, was emerging into power after a long struggle with the once omnipotent Cholas. The bitterness of their battle could not have left the Hoysalas with great love or admiration for the architectural style of their arch foes. The Hoysalas racially too had greater affinity with the north and the Chola buildings held no orthodox sanctity for them. Rather the north Indian craftsman under such conditions was more than welcome to make his contribution to the evolution of a new style. However, faced with the equally strong traditions of his Dravidian counterparts, he was not going to be able to freely erect direct copies of Shikharas and Mandapas as he had for the Yadavas in the Deccan. His contribution perforce had to be of a muted and subtle nature. This fortuitous meeting of master craftsmen brought up in the traditions of the two great styles of Hindu architecture, the northern and the southern resulted in a third, classified as that of the Hoysalas. There must have been a fine spirit of co-operation between the masters, for the style that emerged is neither mere plagiarism of conflicting symbols nor an unseemly clash of two styles. Rather features of the two are subtly merged together into novel forms that have a distinct and refreshing flavour all their own. The wheel had beautifully come the full circle. It was this very region that more than 700 years ago under the Chalukyas, had seen the birth literally side by side, of the pre-eminent features of the northern and southern styles, the Shikhara and the Vimana. Now the builders were back at it again evolving yet another style by the merging together of what may be called the two mother styles.

## THE TEMPLES OF ITTAGI AND GADAG

The synthesis that emerged is seen in its early experimental forms on the fringes of the Hoysala kingdom, which was centred around ancient Dwarsamudra in modern Mysore. It is obvious from even a glance at the various temples at Ittagi, Gadag and Lakhundi that the northern craftsman's most conspicuous contribution to the synthesis was the change he wrought in the form of the tower over the cella. The marked horizontal tiers of the tower were submerged into a profile,

196. A typical vimana shikhara of the Ittagi Dharwar style.

imbued with some of the sensuous grace of the north Indian shikhara. The numerous recesses and chases of the base were carried up into the tower of the newly evolved "Vimana-Shikhara" giving it in plan a form more curvilinear than the Vimana and yet not quite the pronounced parabolic profile of the Shikhara (Fig. 196). The typical circular shafts of the columns of these temples were turned out from a stone lathe, surely suggested by the craftsmen who had moulded similar ones for the mandapas of Gujarat. The repeated application of the motif of the Indo-Aryan shikhara on the walls of the temples is rather forced and incongruous. Gradually this hybrid development of Ittagi and Gadag matured into an identifiable style, challenging the pristine beauty of either of its generic sources. Soon it was acceptable even to the imperial Hoysala rulers at their capital city Dwarasamudra, who perceived in it the potential to rival the more orthodox southern building style of the Cholas and Pandyas.

# THE FAMOUS STAR-SHAPED TEMPLES

To highlight the distinctiveness of their temples, the architects, with due encouragement of the Hoysala kings flamboyantly set about evolving entirely new patterns for their places of worship. Firstly, they planned temples and shrines, within which were situated more than one central garbhagriha or inner cella. These cella, even up to five in number in some temples, were grouped along one end of a large common mandapa. Further the plan of each of these cellas was an elaborate star shape, seemingly defying the sanctity invested in the square by the Hindu art canons. On analysis, however, one finds that the builders had derived even their complex stellar outline from the purity of the square (Fig. 197). This was achieved by rotating the square around its fixed centre, and turning its diagonal through a series of equal angles. The resulting outline of the intersecting corners of so many superimposed squares emerges as a star. The number of its points and their proportions could be varied merely by changing the angle through which the diagonal was turned at every step. By this ingenious device the artist paid due technical deference to the orthodoxy of the square and, at the same time, added a new dimension to temple planning. He was obviously so pleased with his innovation that even the platform over which the temple was raised, echoed the outline of the cella. The towers crowning the various cellas acquired a bell-like profile which was a streamlined version of the "Shikhara-Vimana" that had been evolved by the builders of Ittagi and Dharwar. The Mandapa remained the familiar cross shaped pillared hall. It was distinguished however by the circular shafts of the columns, which emerge now straight from the artistic hands of the lathe cutter, adorned with a series of parallel almost knife-like edges of various shapes.

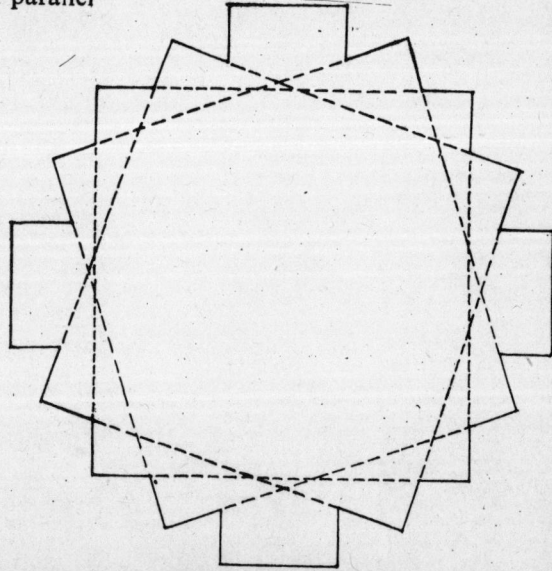

**197.** Revolutions of the square around its centre give rise to a star like profile.

**198.** The knife like edges and the horizontal delineation of the columns of the Hoysala temples.

## TEMPLES OF DUCTILE CHLORITE SCHIST

To build temples of such complexity with unwieldy blocks of sandstone would have been a formidable task indeed. However, a material easier to work with was readily available—a closely textured chlorite schist which was soft when quarried but turned to adamant hardness on exposure to air. This special quality made it the ideal medium for the expression of the elaborate architectonics of the Hoysala builders. The cutters turned blocks of the chlorite schist on a lathe to reduce them to circular shafts. These were invested with a profusion of concave and convex mouldings with almost knife-like edges. The squat horizontality so acquired by these columns (Fig. 198) became the theme of the entire elaborate decorative scheme, from the stylobate of the base to the apex of the bell like tower.

199. Plan view of the 12th century Channa Keshava at Belur.

The Hoysala king Vishnuwardhan is credited with the rebuilding of the old capital of Dwarasamudra, naming it Halebid (Hale—old and Bidu—capital). He is reputed to have initially commissioned his chief architect, the legendary Janaka Acharya to build a temple to the God Channa Keshava (Fig. 199) at Velapura (modern Belur). Though the temple is built around a single shrine, Janaka Acharya incorporated into it all the other essentials of the Hoysala style—star-shaped shrine and platform, bell shaped towers, and pillared mandapas (Fig. 200). Each of the twenty-eight openings between the pillars of the mandapa were later closed up with a trellis work of a rather incongruous design. This was meant to provide privacy for the Brahmins watching the rituals, particularly the highly seductive dancing of the "devadasis." The mandapa of this temple has one of the most beautiful circular stone platforms. Over the centuries it has acquired a lustrous polish from the incessant dancing feet of the exponents of the famous Indian classical dance, the Bharata Natyam. The entire temple is set within a vast rectangular enclosure of 440 ft × 360 feet (134 m × 110 m) to which the traditional gopurams were added at a later date.

200. A column in the Channa Keshava at Somnathpur (1250 A.D.).

201. View, great temple Halebid (1150 A.D.).

## THE CITY OF HALEBID

Carried away by his great religious fervour and immense faith in Janaka Acharya, the same king commissioned an even more elaborate form of the Belur temple. This, the Great Hoysalasvara temple, became the focus of the capital city of Halebid. It is a temple even larger and richer than its predecessor at Belur. The architect proceeded to duplicate his effort at Belur by laying out (Fig. 201) at Halebid two identical temples, parallel to each other connected only at their transepts. Each temple has in addition its own Nandi mandapa detached from the main body of the shrine.

## SCULPTURAL ARCHITECTONICS OF JANAK ACHARYA

Here at Halebid, the master Indian sculptor working with the tactile material of the chlorite schist carved out the most fitting climax to the centuries of his art in India. Virtually not an inch of this vast composition escaped his chisel. The walls of the Hoyselasvara suggest the "analogy of a voluminous, constantly unrolling illustrated scroll," the entire elevation (Fig. 202) being a "scheme of closely crafted continuous mouldings, borders, friezes, cornices and bands of statuary carried all around the building." The richness of the sculpture is so awe inspiring that one scarcely notices the lack of the bell shaped towers over the cellas. These were either never completed or having been constructed around a core of brick were easily desecrated later. Profusely covered with such masterpieces of sculpture as it is, the "Halebid Temple and the Parthenon are probably the two extremes of the architectural art of the world." The one revels in the cold purity of its architectural form and the other in the warm complexity of its sculptural architectonics.

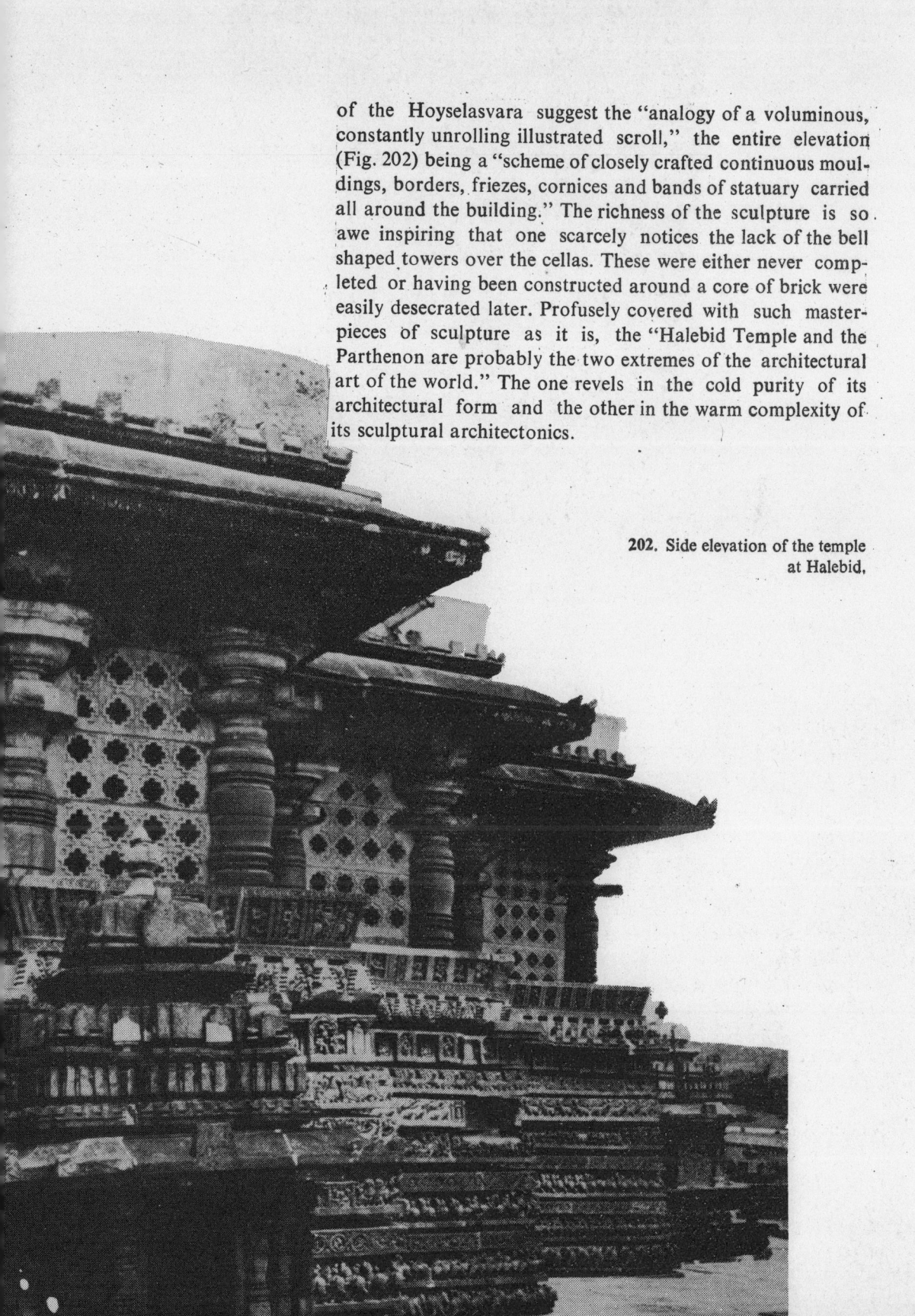

202. Side elevation of the temple at Halebid.

203. The bell-shaped tower and plan of the Prasana Channa Keshava at Somnathpur.

## KESAVA AT SOMNATHPUR

The most complete extant example of the Hoysala builders art is, however, the Prasanna Channa Kesava in Somnathpur (Fig. 203) near modern Bangalore, built by Vardhana in A.D. 1270. Set inside a rectangular courtyard the temple consists of a symmetrical arrangement of triple shrines at the end of a rectangular Mandapa and Navranga(being only another regional term for a dancing hall). It is the only example of Hoysala art that has retained its three bell like towers in a well preserved form.

Not entirely content with a stellar plan for the cellas later builders attempted to transform the plan of the Navranga mandapa also into the shape of a star in the Dumbal Temple at Dosappa. This first experiment could not be elaborated upon, since the collapse of the Hoysala dynasty in the century 1326 A.D. cried halt to the work of the Hindu craftsmen in the Karnataka. Even if the Muslim invasion of the South had not eroded the power of the Hoysalas, whether the Hindu craftsman could possibly have excelled himself beyond the "prodigal plastic manifestations of his art" at Halebid, Belur and Somnathpur, is indeed a moot point.

# 21

# Vijayanagar— the last great glory

## Architecture of Hampi

THE Sultans of Delhi, content with their nominal conquest of the Deccan, established a Turkish Governor at Daulatabad and retired to more urgent Imperial business in their capital city of Delhi. The Governor, true to tradition, followed the familiar pattern of revolt, and at the earliest opportunity proclaimed himself King Bahman Shah with his capital at Gulbarga in modern Mysore. He was, however, unable to expand his empire in the South since the two Hindu Kingdoms—one centred around Warangal (modern Andhra) and the other at Hastnavati (modern Hampi), were not altogether obliging. Ultimately, the Sultans sent armies from Delhi to reclaim their Kingdom in the South. In the process they carried back two Warangal princes, Harihara and Bukka to Delhi. The princes were persuaded to convert to Islam, and sent back, charged with the mission of establishing the Sultan's authority.

Harihara astutely got himself crowned King of Hampi and was even accepted back into the Hindu fold. This unique change was achieved through a Brahmin accomplice who, by the usual Hindu religious mumbo jumbo, claimed divine and infalliable rights for Harihara.

Harihara proved to have been well schooled in the arts of intrigue at the Muslim courts of Delhi. Ably aided by Bukka and proclaiming independence from his Muslim overlords, he went about the task of consolidating his newly acquired Empire. A new empire, of course, could be proclaimed only through a new capital city. For strategic reasons, Harihara decided to expand the existing town of Hampi, situated though it was on "a tossed and tumbled jungle of sunblasted stones with only limited open spaces intervening." Rather they took advantage of the ready availability of material from the very site of construction as it were, and completed the first phase of expansion in a short period of seven years.

## COAST TO COAST EMPIRE

The empire founded by Harihara continued to grow. Within a period of hundred years it stretched from the eastern to the western sea-coast. Such a vast domain was defended by an enormous army "comprising a million fighting troops in which are included 35,000 cavalry in armour." Curiously enough, though horses were the mainstay of such a force, the Indians never took seriously to horse breeding. They purchased them from Portuguese traders who had by now entrenched themselves in Goa. The Portuguese, apart from trading "Arab

The so called Soolai Bazar, one of the remains of the once grand city of Vijayanagar of the 16th century A.D.

horses, velvets, Damasks and satins" for "jewels and pagodas which be ducats of gold," had carefully established friendly relations with Hindu Vijayanagar, the Muslims being their major rivals for control of the trade across the Arabian sea. Hampi meanwhile continued to prosper and in keeping with the series of conquests and victories grew into the famous Vijayanagar—the city of Victory.

By the time of King Devaraja II, less than 100 years after its founding by Harihara, Nicolo Conti, an Italian traveller visited Vijayanagar in 1420. He estimated (somewhat exaggeratedly it would seem), that "the circumference of the city be sixty miles." He was "much impressed by the strength of the fortifications which were carried up the hills so as to enclose the valleys at their base." These valleys were watered by constructing a huge dam in the Tungabhadra river, which conveyed water to the city through an aqueduct fifteen miles in length, cut out of the solid rock for a distance of several miles." The outlying areas of the "tossed and tumbled jungle" were transformed into cultivated fields and pastures, well stocked with flocks and herds. "The city was therefore so well supplied that it could stand a siege for an almost indefinite period."

## THE MARVELS AND BLANDISHMENTS OF VIJAYANAGAR

This is amply borne out by the remains of the fortifications of the city; we can see that the builders had left little to chance. They have been described by a contemporary Abdur Razzaq, an Ambassador sent by Sultan Shahrukh of Herat to the Zamorin of Calicut. After travelling across "streets as wide as tourney's" he found that Vijayanagar was "so built that it has seven fortified walls, one within the other. The seventh fortress is placed in the centre of the others and occupies ground ten times greater than the chief market of Herat. In that is situated the palace of the King. From the northern gate of the outer fortress to the southern gate is a distance of two statute "parasangs" (about 7 or 8 miles) and the same with respect to the distance between the eastern and western gates. From the third to the seventh fortress, shops and bazaars are closely crowded together."

The best of the bazaars, true to the tradition of a thriving Indian city of the middle ages, were the houses of the devadasis, "the (euphemistic) handmaids of the gods." The prostitutes quarters, in fact, was "one of the sights of the

204. The myriads of columns in the hall of the Vithala temple at Vijayanagar

capital." The splendour of their houses and the beauty of the hearts ravishers their blandishment and ogles" were to Razak "beyond description." Apart from providing for the sexual appetites of the inhabitants of Vijayanagar the tax on the proceeds of the brothels, if one is to believe Razak, paid for 2000 policemen whose salary amounted to 12,000 pafanams daily.

## THE PALACE OF KRISHNADEVARAJA

Under the rule of King Krishnadevaraja, a contemporary of King Henry VIII, the city was visited by Pae, a Portuguese traveller to whom it seemed "as large as Rome and very beautiful to the sight." It consisted of over 100,000 houses and must at the time have had a population of over half a million. The king's palace "stood in an enclosure that contained thirty four streets, in the heart of the city. The private apartments of the palace were in a separate building known as the house of victory. One of them was panelled with ivory from top to bottom. The pillars were made of rosewood decorated with flowers and lotuses, all of ivory, and well executed, so that there could not be better."

The King's audience chamber was elevated above the rest. "In this agreeable locality one sees numerous running streams and canals formed of chiselled stone, polished and smooth." The wilderness that the city is today was once covered with "many lime and orange trees, growing so closely together, one to another, that it appears like a thick forest."

## FINANCE AND RELIGION

Such a magnificent Hindu feudal city could not conceivably have existed without the support of the priestly class. King Krishnadevaraja of the 16th century, under whom Vijayanagar reached the climax of its glory, conferred "almost fabulous wealth as endowments on temples and Brahmins." It ensured that the Brahmins would not challenge the rather questionable heredity of the kings from a Muslim convert.

A large part of the endowments went into financing the ever expanding ceremonials of religion. The rituals had become so elaborate that it was no longer possible to contain them within the traditional axially aligned compartments of a temple. The temples of Vijayanagar, thus, are not the unified compositions of the Cholas or the Hoysalas. They are in fact

205. In Vijayanagar, it is some times difficult to tell where nature ends and art begins as in this, the Raghunath temple, built virtually over living rock.

a number of small units, each with its own prescribed function, set rather haphazardly as dictated by the terrain, within a large rectangular enclosure. The basic unit of such a temple conglomerate was a flat roofed hall, supported on a series of elaborately crafted columns.

## NATURE AND ABODES OF GOD

In the temples and palaces of Viajayanagar, often the living rock itself became the foundation of a grand super-structure and "it is sometimes difficult to tell where nature ends and (man-made) art begins" (Fig. 205). The builders have, unintentionally may be, left behind a most graphic record of perfect harmony between art and nature. "The striking, almost planet-like landscape of the region," lives here with the handiwork of man, as if the two were never separate.

206. The mandapa of the Vithala temple capped with the typical double flexured cornice of the Vijayanagar style.

# THE GREAT VITHALA TEMPLE

The Vithala temple (Fig. 206) commissioned by Krishnadevaraja, as late as the beginning of the 16th century, is spread over an area of approximately 500 feet × 300 feet (152 metres × 91 metres). The central part is a series of conjoined pillared halls extending horizontally over a distance of 200 feet (61 metres) but nowhere rising more than 25 feet (7.6 metres). The tower over the garbhagriha, if one was ever erected, has vanished. It was most likely constructed in brick and plaster. Beyond the extensiveness of its conception there is little to commend it, since the temple is devoid of any tangible architectural form. The Hindu craftsmen of Vijayanagar concentrated his energies on the myriads of columns, each of these becoming a miniature architectural composition in itself (Fig. 204). Interposed between the columns is a "half natural, half mythical" relief of a lion, resurrected like a ghost from the ancient Pallava period. Each pillar expands below into a massive pedestal and above into grotesque brackets of gigantic proportions. Any concept of space in the flat roofed halls is devoured by clusters of such columns. Ultimately the halls produce "an effect of bewildering intricacy" rather than comprehensible art. Within the "Kalyana mandapa," attached to the temple, the marriage of gods and goddesses was conducted annually. It is if one can imagine it to be possible, even more elaborately wrought than the main mandapa. Capped by the same "voluptuous double flexured cornice with a turned up outer edge" this hall is held up by twelve piers around a square throne in the centre. The major sculptural relief that stands out from this forestry of columns is an imitation chariot car (Fig. 208) which is wrought from a single block of hard granite. Its stone wheels, lifted a few inches from the ground, actually revolve around their axles.

# TEMPLE OF HAZARI RAM

The same king also commissioned the building of a private chapel, for some curious reason now called the temple of Hazari Ram (Fig. 207). Architecturally, it is as undistinguished as the Vithala but the sculpture "attained an extravagance that has an inevitable suggestion of the grotesque and fanciful." This effect is highlighted by the Amman Shrine at the rear, where for good measure it would seem, the sculptor added the keel roof form of the Buddhist Chaitya hall to the ever expanding chiaruscoro of fanciful shapes.

It would seem as if Hindu architecture in its dying glory was momentarily but rapidly improvising on scenes and memories of its long and distinguished past; a glory that was finally shattered in a great crescendo of violent upheaval. Krishnadevaraja had been succeeded by his son Achyutarya who succumbed to the machinations of his minister Ramaraja. Ramaraja secured the throne in the name of Krishnadevaraja's son, and was for a while successful in his intrigues with the Muslim kings of the Deccan. Due to his growing arrogance, however, the Muslims ultimately formed an alliance to challenge his power.

207. The Hazari Ram temple at Vijayanagar.

208. The ratha of the Vithala temple wrought from a single block of hard granite.

## INTRIGUE AND ISLAMIC TRIUMPH

On the banks of the Kistna, 25 miles from the town of Talikot the 600 guns of the Muslim confederation routed the Vijayanagar army of "between half a million men, besides a multitude of elephants." The victorious Muslim army, after a day's rest attacked the capital city and for a space of 5 months Vijayanagar knew no rest. "Never perhaps in the history of the world had such havoc been wrought on so splendid a city. The magnificent stone carving was smashed to pieces with crow-bars and hammers and where it defied human efforts fires were lit to burst it open. Teeming with a wealthy and industrious population full of plentitude and prosperity one day—the proud capital was (soon) a forlorn ruin inhabited only by tigers and other wild beasts." It was reduced to what Percy Brown 300 years later described as "the striking and almost planet like landscape."

The Empire never quite recovered from the disastrous battle of Talikot. Ramaraja's unfortunate successors were left to rule a sadly diminished kingdom, from Penukoda and Chandagiri. Eventually the Nayaks, tributary leaders of the Vijayanagar Empire, fled deeper into the South to escape the wrath of Muslim invasions.

# 22

## Nayaks of the Deep South

### Temple cities of Madurai and Rameswaram

VIJAYANAGAR epitomises the last flamboyant outburst of Hindu power against Islam's inexorable advance into the Southern peninsula. Once it crumbled, the Nayaks, representing Hindu rule in its dying phase, receded to their capital city of Madurai deep in the South. The more orthodox Hindu craftsmen followed them, seeking refuge in the fading glory of their feudal lords.

**THE TEMPLE BECOMES A FORT**

With the growing uncertainties of temporal power, the building of new architectural masterpieces to the "glory of God" was hardly possible. There was little time, inspiration, or spirit for the blossoming of fresh artistic ideas. Building craftsmen had even under the aegis of the powerful Vijayanagar empire, kept themselves busy in erecting hall after hall, of myriads of columns. They were quite content now to merely elaborate on the theme. The requirements of the keepers of the temple also required buildings more of a defensive and essential character rather than of an innovative nature. It was more practical to protect the deity from the defiling invasions of Islam, than to attempt to create new exuberant forms for its house. The temple builders' art was virtually reduced to throwing a series of sacrosanct battlements around the divine presence, punctuated by well guarded gateways at the cardinal points.

Thus, the great temple of Srirangam near Trichurapalli (Fig. 211) acquired several concentric rings of growth. Not

211. Plan of the temple at Srirangam that acquired several prakramas and concentric walls over a period of hundred of years to grow into a temple city.

210. The great curvilinear gopuram of Madurai soaring almost 50 metre into the sky (1600 A.D.).

merely over a decade or a century, but more like a town and a city, over a period of more than 500 years. During the Chola's time it probably was no more than a village shrine consisting of the usual cella and mandapa. For various reasons it gained great religious popularity. The space within the walled enclosure surrounding the cella had become too small for conducting group ceremonies and accommodating the growing number of pilgrims. Nevertheless both for sacred and practical reasons it was not to be pulled down. The necessary additional space could have been provided by a courtyard or hall outside the front entrance. This however would have placed the new ancillaries at an inconvenient distance from the inner shrine. A more reasonable solution was to throw another concentric wall around the existing one. New structures could now be built in the space between the two parallel walls. This ensured that the additional halls were conveniently located more or less equi-distant from the old inner shrine.

## AND THE FORT BECOMES A CITY

Over a period of time with the accretion of greater religious merit and pilgrims arriving in thousands to attend festivities stretching over days, the temple precincts needed to be enlarged further. The precedents of the methodology of growth had now been established. More space was acquired and yet another even larger concentric wall came up. With the many elaborate rituals to be performed in the vicinity of the central shrine, the original open court surrounding the garbhagriha was completely roofed over. The sacred image of the presiding deity, that in any case could be only dimly perceived in the uncertain light of myriads of lamps, acquired an even more mysterious and sacred quality (Fig. 212).

More people were attracted to the wonder temple. Sacred tanks, for them to bathe themselves in before confronting their gods, were built. Two of these, one a conventional rectangular one, representing the sun and a semi-circular one representing the moon, became the part of another courtyard of the ever growing temple of Srirangam. The staff attached to such a temple naturally increased manifold and a large part of it lived in the many houses built within the many temple walls.

More space was added by the well established pattern; another wall, another set of gopurams, more halls and consequently longer corridors. Scores of rooms, cella and chambers were built as dictated by their functional use rather than

212. The mysterious and sacred inner sanctum of the great temple city.

architectural harmony. The only two elements that conformed to an architectural pattern, in this great crescendo of haphazard growth were the surrounding wall and gopurams. The former were inevitably concentric to each other and the latter invariably built along the cardinal axes. Over the years, the core of the Srirangam temple enclosure of 80 feet × 240 feet (24 metres × 73 metres) had grown into a massive temple city of 2880 × 2475 feets (878 metres × 754 metres) sprawling over an area of more than a quarter square mile. Ultimately, the rather fortutious design of a temple as a series of concentric fortifications adorned with massive gopurams became an accepted "style" of temple building.

213. Plan of the Meenakshi temple at Madurai enclosing two shrines within its prakrama (1600 A.D.).

## THE MINAKSHI TEMPLE AT MADURAI

Thus, the Minakshi temple, in Madurai (Fig. 213), built in a few decades, was right from its inception, designed as a series of concentric courtyards or "prakarmas" as they came to be classified. The ever alert Brahmin keepers also seized this opportunity to protect their precious god with rings of receding sanctity and security. Spaces around the shrine, the new "prakramas" were endowed with diminishing religious value directly proportional to their distance from the deity in the inner shrine. The outermost circle accommodated edifices of a practical rather than spiritual nature—accounts offices, dormitories for pilgrims, kitchens, shops dealing in the essential items for the rituals, maintenance workshops and parking areas for the growing number of wooden festive chariots. The lower class menials who were needed to service these areas, were permitted only into the outlying areas.

The inner prakramas contained pavilions for devotional singing and story telling, bathing tanks for ritual ablutions, and guest houses for important visitors. To such enclosures only caste Hindus were allowed. In the inner most courts were the kitchens of the Brahmins, the pavilions for the dancing girls and the treasury, over both of which the Brahmin kept a watchful eye. Admittance to these was often restricted to the upper caste only. Even the chosen few allowed to have "darshan" of the deity, could wear only a brief loin cloth and nothing else—likely to make it impossible for them to hide away and pilfer the many valuable treasures of the temple within the folds of their clothes. The actual cella containing the graven image of the god was of course open only to the officiating priest and none else—not even royalty.

## HALLS OF MANY PILLARS

With temple building beginning to approximate more to city and town planning, the building craftsman's art was restricted to the erection of pavilions, halls and gopurams, the subsequent ones larger and more gracious than the preceding.

The largeness of one of the flat roofed halls, commissioned by Vinayak Mudali, a minister of the Nayak kings, necessitated the setting up of an elaborate stone cutters factory. Columns upon columns and beams upon beams of a standard design were unendingly churned out of this factory. The hall situated within the Minakshi temple (Fig. 214) complex, needed 985 pillars to support its roof measuring 240 feet × 250 feet

(73 metres × 76 metres). This is the famous "hall of thousand pillars" and little else. Today, ironically enough, the hall, surely one of the more arid products of Indian craftsmanship is a museum of drawings and photographs of the entire gamut of the 1200 years of temple architecture of the south. Evidently, the builders and the patrons were undaunted by the monotony of their productions, drawing consolation from the massive size of their building ventures. They took seven years to build another even larger, even less distinguished 330 feet (100.5 metres) deep Choultri; this time at the command of the last Nayak, Tirumalai, who had it built outside the main precinct of the Madurai temple south of the outermost gopurams.

## THE SOARING GOPURAMS

Even the gopurams had in many ways become a rather mechanical and repetitive form, growing only in size. The potential of its large surfaces, however, was exploited to some extent by the indefatigable Indian sculptor. In its earlier stages the profile of the gopuram was a rigid pyramidal tower, its horizontal tiers clearly defined by a series of vertical pilasters and horizontal cornices. Inevitably, however, the Hindu sculptor infused into it a more plastic quality, by making its profiles curvilinear (Fig. 210). Subsequently the pilasters and cornices lost their sharpness and became absorbed into one large amorphous jumbled mass of sculpture. The outermost more than 150 feet (48 m.) high gopurams of the Minakshi temple are the finest examples of this type of gopuram. Once completed in the 17th century, the temple city of Madurai became the model for temple buildings in the South. Many old village shrines expanded into temple cities. As a result there is hardly a temple of any religious consequence in the South which has not been surrounded by prakarmas, entered through a series of axially aligned gopurams. Though evolving on much the same pattern as Srirangam, some acquired special distinctive features of their own.

## THE CORRIDORS OF RAMESHWARAM

214. A part of the hall of thousand pillars of the temple of Madurai.

Rameshwaram, situated on the tip of a narrow strip of land jutting out into the sea, for instance is a maze of generously proportioned pillared verandahs. The temple is not only surrounded by corridors, (Fig. 215), but is connected to the outer entrances by transverse covered passage ways. To build these, masons patiently crafted and erected massive square columns, sufficient to roof avenues of these, aggregating more than 3000 feet (914 metres) in length. Rameshwaram has thereby acquired the dubious architectural record of possessing the longest corridors in the world. The Jambukeswar, within a mile of Srirangam, on the other hand, has probably the most massive and elaborate shafts and brackets for its numerous columns. These are more like elaborate inverted pyramids than mere pillars. The Shiva temple at Chidambaram boasts of a central shrine that is in the shape of a chariot, while the temple at Srivilliputtur is entered through a gopuram of 14 distinct storeys, soaring over 200 feet (61 metres) into the skies.

In spite of the many individual variations and gimmicks and world records, the essence of Hindu temple architecture in the South from the 16th to the 19th century is contained in a series of concentric walls, gopurams of varying size, and halls and corridors of thousands of columns. Even the impressive skyline of gopurams of ascending heights, (Fig. 216), is due more to fortuitious circumstances than planned strategy, unlike the preconceived intention of the pylons of Egyptian temples, which they resemble.

As we have seen, Indian architecture, for over a period of 300 years under the last Hindu lords of the South, did not show even a glimpse of a new form, a new idea. The keepers of the temples were content to surround prakarma with prakarma filled haphazardly with pillared halls connected by tedious corridors, relieved here and there by gopurams. Mercifully, this monotonous building activity could not be carried out endlessly. Whether the spread of Islam or the bankruptcy of Brahmin thought brought about the end, is a moot point; most likely a bit of both since the southernmost tip of India never really passed under direct Muslim control, nor has the Brahmin, even to date, quite lost his grip over the Hindu mind. Architecturally, however, the Hindu temple of the 18th and 19th century had become literally a fortress, that had drawn up the bridge to new ideas.

Building craftsmen though, had not lost their intrinsic skills. Rather the life giving sap of new challenges had dried up, since the priest was content with altogether stereotyped forms. With Hindu temporal power also at a low ebb, patronage for the building of glorious monuments was no longer at hand. A number of orthodox Hindu craftsmen must have remained loyal to their religion. Some were occupied in renovating and refurbishing old Hindu temples and some in building small village shrines, here and there in the countryside. A good many others, either more loyal to their craft than to religious dogma, or through compulsion, took up the new challenge; that of building monuments for their new Muslim overlords. The north, which centuries earlier had succumbed to Muslim domination, was already bustling with activity. Given another set of rulers, another concept, the Indian craftsmen set gamely about his task of erecting palaces, tombs and mosques.

Over the ensuing centuries, he convincingly proved that his craft was an undying one. It continued to flourish just as much under Muslim as it had under Hindu hegemony. The Muslim period though, is another era in the history of the building arts of India.

215. A portion of the more than 1000 metre length of corridors, that are the major feature of the temple at Rameswaram, of the 17th century.

# Bibliography

BASHAM, A.L., *The Wonder that was India*, Sidgwick & Jackson, London 1954.

BATLEY, C., *Design Development of Indian Architecture*, John Murray, London 1934.

BROWN, P., *Indian Architecture (Buddhists and Hindu Period)*, Taraporevala & Sons, Bombay 1965.

CUNNINGHAM, A., *Archaeological Survey of India*, Vols. I—XXIII, Simla, Calcutta 1903-30.

EDWARDES, M., *Indian Temples and Palaces*, Paul Hamlyn, London 1959.

FERGUSSON, J., *History of Indian and Eastern Architecture*, John Murray, London 1910.

GOETZ, H, *Five Thousand Years of Indian Art*, Methuen, London 1959.

HAVELL. E.B., *The Ancient and Medieval Architecture of India*, John Murray, London 1915; and *The Ideals of Indian Art*, John Murray, London 1920.

KRAMRISCH, S., *The Hindu Temple*, University of Calcutta Press, Calcutta 1946.

LAL, K., *Temples and Sculptures of Bhubaneswar*, Arts & Letters, New Delhi 1970.

MARSHALL, J., *Annual Reports of the Archaeological Survey of India*, Calcutta, 1903-30 and *Mohenjodaro and the Indus Civilization*, London 1931.

NEHRU, J., *The Discovery of India*, Meridian Books, London 1946.

PIGGOT, S., *Pre-historic India*, Penguin Books, Harmondsworth 1950.

RAWLINSON, H.G., *India, A Short Cultural History*, The Cresset Press, London 1937.

ROWLAND, B., *The Art and Architecture of India*, Penguin Books, Harmondsworth, 1953.

THAPAR, R., *A History of India*, Penguin Books, Harmondsworth, 1966.

VOLWAHSEN, A., *Living Architecture of India*, MacDonald, London, 1970.

WHEELER, R.E.M., *Early India and Pakistan*, Thames and Hudson, London 1959; and *The Indus Civilization*, Cambridge University Press, Cambridge. 1953.

ZIMMER, H., *The Art of Indian Asia*, Oxford University Press, London 1968.

# Glossary

*Amalaka*: A flat fluted disc like stone representative of the holy fruit "amala", usually at the summit of the Shikhara.
*Antevasika*: A resident in a hostel.
*Anda*: Literally "egg", the hemispherical dome of the stupa.
*Antralay*: Entrance chamber in front of shrines.
*Ardha Mandapa*: Chamber before the main "mandapa" or hall
*Aryaka*: A Buddhist worshipful column.
*Asana*: A sitting platform, bench or throne.
*Bazaar*: Market, shopping street.
*Bhog Mandapa*: Hall in a temple where food from donors is supposed to be blessed by the enshrined deity.
*Brahma*: The Hindu God Supreme.
*Chaitya*: From "chita" a pyre but later a Buddhist sanctuary and ultimately the Buddhist hall of worship.
*Chaultri*: Pillared dormitory halls outside Dravidian temple.
*Chattra*: Literally umbrella; a honorific canopy at the apex of the Buddhist stupa.
*Chuna*: Lime, from the Chunar quarries in Bihar the chief north Indian source of building lime.
*Dagoba*: Simhalese terminology for the Buddhist stupa.
*Deul*: From Deva—"God", signifying the inner sanctum but in Orissa applicable to the temple as a whole.
*Garbhagriha*: Literally "the womb", the most sacred inner sanctum of the temple where the deity is enshrined.
*Ghat*: Platforms or steps at edge of lake or river water.
*Ghats*: Popular term for the mountainous territory south of the Deccan Plateau and in the pennisular portion between the Bay of Bengal and the Arabian sea.
*Gopuram*: Monumental South Indian temple gateway.
*Harmika*: The square platform at the apex of the Stupa sometimes surrounded by a railing and from top of which the honorific umbrella rises.
*Hinayana*: The earliest form of Buddhism that did not include the worship of images of the Buddha as a God.
*Indra*: The ideal warrior God of the Hindu pantheon.
*Jagmohan*: Orissan terminology for hall in front of the sanctuary.
*Jina*: Mythological reformer in the Jain religion.
*Kailasa*: The haven of the Hindu God Shiva.
*Kalasa*: Literally vase, religious inverted pot installed over the amalaka as a finial for the Shikhara.
*Kalyan Mandapa*: Hall of "marriage of the Gods" in South Indian temples.
*Lat*: Pillar or column.
*Mahal*: Palace, hall.
*Mahayana*: Later development of Buddhism that accepted Buddha as Saviour and permitted the worship of its image.

*Mandapa*: Large hall generally the chambers preceding the inner sanctum of the Hindu temple.
*Mandir*: Temple.
*Medhi*: Terrace or platform.
*Nandi*: The sacred bull.
*Nat Mandir*: Dancing hall in Hindu temple particularly in Orissan terminology.
*Navranga*: Central hall of temple particularly in Gujarat temples.
*Panchayatna*: Temple consisting of a central shrine and four subsidiary shrines at the corners.
*Pradakshinapath*: Processional ambulatory passage particularly Buddhist, around the stupa.
*Prakrama*: Open courtyard particularly the ring of courtyards in South Indian temples.
*Purana Kalasa*: Symbolic vase of plenty, pot and foliage motif of column capitals of the Gupta period.
*Ratha*: Literally car or chariot. Particularly car used in Hindu processional festivals, sometimes also signifying temple.
*Sabha Mandapa*: Assembly hall.
*Santhagara*: Village or town meeting hall.
*Seni*: Guilds.
*Shikhara*: Literally mountain peak but generally the spire or tower over north Indian Hindu temple.
*Silpa Sastra*: Ancient Indian treatise on architecture, building and allied arts.
*Stambha*: Column or pillar.
*Sthapati*: Master craftsman.
*Stupa*: Originally a folk funerary mound but crystallised by Buddhism into a hemispherical form to enshrine a sacred spot or relic.
*Surya*: The Hindu Sun God.
*Suryavanshi*: Rajput tribes claiming descent from the Sun God.
*Tirathankara*: Jain religious reformers.
*Torana*: Gateway, particularly the ceremonial gates at the cardinal points of the stupa.
*Trimurti*: Sculpture embodying three Gods, particularly Brahma, the creator; Vishnu, the preserver and Shiva, the destroyer.
*Urusringa*: A half profile shikhara superimposed over main shikhara particularly in the Khajuraho style.
*Vastu Sastra*: Ancient Indian treatise on the "Rules of Architecture."
*Vedas*: Ancient texts embodying the essence of the Aryan religious life in the form of mantras or chants to be recited at religious ceremonies.

*Vedi*: Altar.
*Vedica*: Buddhist railing generally demarcating a sacred area.
*Vihara*: Residence for Buddhist or Jain monks.
*Vimana*: Pyramidical tower over the inner sanctum generally of South Indian temples.

# Index

Ahimsa 27
Aihole 81 101, 102
Ajanta 74, 76, 81
Ajatashatru 22
Ali Masjid Stupa 65
Amravati Stupa 49
Ambernath temple 203
Amla 91, 178
Anant Vasudeva Temple 159
Anda 41
Angkor Vat 97
Antevasikas 173
Arykas 49
Aryan 13
Aryan carpenter 15
Aryan religious life 16
Aryan Village 14, 15
Ashoka, the great 27
Assyrians 28
Avantipur 133
Avantiswami temple 133
Avantivarman 132
Ayodhya 17
Aztecs 28

Bada 178
Badami 101, 109
Barabar 33
Belur 208, 209
Bhaja 50, 51
Bharhut 67
Bhattiprolu 47
Bhima 108
Bhitargaon temple 86
Bhubaneswar 142 152
Bhumi 178
Brahminism 21, 37
Brihidesyara temple 193
Buddhism 22
Budh Gaya 94, 95, 96

Cave architecture 32, 52
Chaitya (halls, caves) 35, 44
Chalukya 101
Champa 17
Chankya 25
Chandelas 147
Chandragupta Maurya 24, 70
Chanhudaro 13
Channa Keshave temple 208
Chopra 178
Chatra 42
Chezarala 71

Chidambaram 229
Cholas 118, 193
Choultri 228
Chunnar 30

Deogarh 82, 90, 128
Dhamek Stupa 95
Dharamaraj Ratha 108, 112, 113
Dharwar 206
Doab 14
Dosappa 213
Dumbal temple 213
Durga temple 101, 84
Dwarasamudra 204, 205, 208

Egyptians 28
Elapura 121
Elephanta cave 119
Ellora 121
Erotic sculpture 190

Fire temple 61
Flying toranas 182
Frescoes of Ajanta 75

Gadag 204, 205
Gandhara 61
Ganesh Ratha 108
Gangaikonda Cholapuram 196
Garhwal 130
Gautam, the Buddha 212
Gaya 71
Ghantsala 48
Ghorapuri 118
Ghumli 161
Gopuram 199, 200, 209
Gudiada 47
Gupta 81

Halebid 208, 210
Hall of 1000 pillars 228
Hampi 215
Harappa 3, 4, 9, 10, 11
Harihara 215, 217
Harmika 42
Harsha 93
Hastınapur 17
Hastinavati 215
Hazari Ram Temple 220
Hinayana 60
Hinduism 69, 70
Hoysalas 204
Hoysalesvara temple 210

Indraprastha 17
Indus Valley 4, 9, 10, 12, 13
Ittagi 204, 205, 206

Jagannath Temple 154
Jaina, architectural style 168
Jainism 22
Jambu Keswar 229
Janak Acharya 210
Jandial 61
Jangha 178

Kailasa Temple 121, 123
Kalasa 91, 178
Kilibangan 10
Kalinga 27, 142
Kalayani 197
Kanauj 125, 126
Kanchipuram 112, 116, 118
Kandariya Mahadev temple 187
Kanishka 62
Karli 54, 55, 56, 76
Kashi 17
Kashmir 130
Kathiawar 159
Kaushambi 17, 19
Kayal 197
Khajuraho 147, 149, 151
Kiradu 159
Konarak 183
Krishadevaraja 217, 219
Kusingara 19

Ladkhan temple 82, 84, 102, 103
Lakhundi 204
Lakshmana temple 149
Lalithaditya 130
Lauriya Nandgarh 31
Le orbusier 174, 176
Leonardo da Vinci 176
Lingaraja temple 154, 155
Lomas Rishi 33
Lothal 3, 10

Madura 227
Mahaballipuram 107, 107
Mahabharata 117
Mahavira 22, 168
Mahayana 60, 63
Makrani
Mandala 174, 175
Martand 135
Mathura 62, 67

Middle path 22
Minakshi temple 227
Modhera 181, 182
Modular 176
Mohenjadaro 3, 4, 6, 9, 10, 11
Mount Abu 165
Muktesvara temple 145

Nagarjuni 33
Nalanda 71, 96
Narshimdeva 185
Navlakha temples 161
Nayaks 223
Nepal 130
Nirvana 22

Osian 128, 152

Pagodas 67
Palitana 168
Pallavas 106
Pandyas 198
Papanath temple 113, 114
Pattadakal 113
Parasurameswara temple 144
Pataliputra 25
Peshawar 62
Pida 178
Pradkshina path 38
Prassana Channa Keshava 213
Puri 152
Purusha 176
Purushpura 62
Pyramids 28

Rahapaga 178
Rajaraja 193
Rajendra I 195
Rajgriha 17
Rajrani temple 156
Ramayana 17
Rameshwaranm 229
Rastrakutas 113
Rathas 107
Rupar 10

Sabha 16
Sacrificial altars 90
Sagala 59
Sahdeva Rath 108
Samiti 19
Sanchi 37, 45, 67, 77

Sanskrit 70
Santhagar 81
Sargom 3
Sarnath 22, 71, 94, 95, 96
Sas Bahu temple 162
Sejakpur 161
Shankaracharya 131
Shatrunjaya 168
Shikhara 91
Shore temple 111
Shrasvati 17
Shungas 37
Sirkap 60
Somnathpur 213
Somnath temple 159
Srinagar 131
Srirangam 223
Stambhas 30
Stonehenge 30
Stupa 29
Sun temple, Konark 183
Sun Temple Mqrtand 132
Sun Temple Modhera 181
Suraj Kund 141
Swastika 42

Takht-Bahi 63, 93
Taxila 22
Teli-ka-Mandir 139-142
Ter 71
Thana 203

Thanjavur 193
Tigawa 77, 79
Tirathankars 166
Toda churches 89
Toran 40
Trimoorti 121
Trimuli Nayak 228

Vaikuntha Perumal 116
Vaital Deul 142
Vastupurushmandala 176
Vastushastra 172
Vedic Relition 21
Vedika 39
Velapura 208
Viharas 43, 74
Vijaynagar 216
Vimala Shah Temple 165
Vimana 104
Vimana-Shikara 205
Vinayak Mudali 227
Virupaksha temple 116
Vishnuwardhan 208
Vithala temple 219

Western Ghats 118

Yadavas 203

Ziggaruts 28
Zimbabwe 39

298 SH   BR  1293
05/25/95  32550